Praise for
Divine Renovation

"If you care about the local church, you care about its health and renewal. That's why I'm so thankful for Fr. Simon Lobo and his mentor, Fr. James Mallon. They are catalysts for renewal that is spreading across the Church, breaking down traditional categories and boundaries. This book will take you on a journey to revitalization, both personal and congregational, which is exactly the kind of thing our churches and its leaders need."
—**Carey Nieuwhof**, founding pastor, Connexus Church

"The Church has a great need of people like Fr. Simon Lobo speaking very practically about how to transform parish life into all that it can and should be in the 21st century. With great humility, a sense of humor, and wisdom, Fr. Lobo offers many pearls of wisdom here."
—**Fr. John Riccardo**, pastor of Our Lady of Good Counsel Parish, Plymouth, Michigan

"When, as his superior at Companions of the Cross, I sent Fr. Simon to Saint Benedict Parish, I asked that he find a creative way to share the wisdom he was learning with our whole community. In response, he began bloglike updates. I am so pleased that they are now adapted to a wider audience. I have absolutely no doubt that they will greatly enrich the ministry of all who implement what they read."
—**Most Rev. Scott McCaig, CC**, Bishop of the Military Ordinariate of Canada

"Every page of this book is a testimony both to the fierce intentionality required to keep first things first in pastoral ministry and the overwhelming faithfulness of God when you do."
—**Brett Powell**, Archbishop's delegate for development and ministries, Archdiocese of Vancouver

"Fr. Simon Lobo documents in a simple, practical way what he has come to learn at Saint Benedict. What makes this book accessible and transferable is after each chapter, he invites the reader to consider, "What do I want you to know? What do I want you to do?" These two considerations help personalize the nuggets of truth and activate them into one's own parish community."
—**André Regnier**, cofounder, Catholic Christian Outreach

"In *Divine Renovation Apprentice*, Fr. Lobo distills the best insights from business leadership, parish renewal strategies, and his own personal experience. A valuable resource for any pastor or parish team embarking on parish renewal."
— **Dr. Bob Rice**, professor of catechetics, Franciscan University of Steubenville, and author of *Between the Savior and the Sea*

"The crisis in parish life is a real and urgent problem for the Church in the West. But the good news is that we don't have to figure out the solutions by ourselves. In our very midst, we are seeing a very small number of incredible and dynamic parishes that shine out as beacons of hope and inspiration. *Divine Renovation Apprentice* gives you the inside look at one of these model parishes."
— **Michael Dopp**, president of Mission of the Redeemer Ministries and founder of the New Evangelization Summit

FOREWORD BY FR. JAMES MALLON

Divine Renovation Apprentice

Learning to Lead a
Disciple-Making Parish

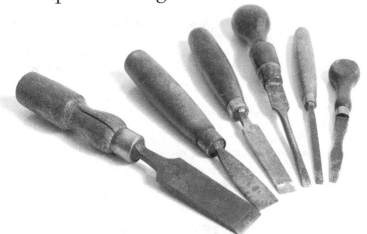

Fr. Simon Lobo, CC

the WORD
among us®
press

Published by The Word Among Us Press
7115 Guilford Drive, Suite 100
Frederick, Maryland 21704
www.wau.org

22 21 20 19 18   1 2 3 4 5

ISBN: 978-1-59325-336-3
eISBN: 978-1-59325-511-4

Cover design by Janaya Seath

Made and printed in the United States of America

Library of Congress Control Number: 2017962847

To Fr. Bob Bedard, CC (1929–2011)
Founder of the Companions of the Cross
*After Jesus himself, you have been my primary
model of priesthood.*

and

to the parishioners and staff of Saint Benedict Parish
and, in a particular way, the original Senior Leadership Team:
Fr. James Mallon, Ron Huntley, Rob McDowell,
and Kate Robinson
*Thank you for apprenticing me in the art of parish leadership.
I still have much to learn.*

Contents

Transforming Culture / 19

Creating a Game Plan / 77

Contents

Leadership Development / 137

Foreword

Fr. James Mallon,
author of *Divine Renovation*

The great Canadian media guru Marshall McCluhan once stated that "the medium is the message." The very existence of this book, *Divine Renovation Apprentice: Learning to Lead a Disciple-Making Parish*, communicates that we can learn something about parish renewal and the art of leadership. Leadership is the gift that unleashes all other gifts within any group of people and within a parish. For too long, however, we have shackled the possibility of successful parishes to charismatic personalities and workaholics, as if only a select few can actually move a parish to a place of health. The reality is that we can learn, contextualize, and apply particular principles that can move a parish to a place of health. This should provide hope to many in the Church.

I believe that God desires, infinitely more than we do, that the Church fulfill the mission entrusted to her by Jesus Christ. Jesus Christ is alive today as much as in the past. The Holy Spirit is blowing as in past ages, and the Word of God still cuts sharper than a two-edged sword. The Eucharist is still the Eucharist, and the sacraments continue to be privileged moments of encounter with the Lord. The essence of what the Church has to offer is still of infinite value, still wondrous and beautiful, and still the answer to the deepest desire of the human heart. In spite of this truth, however, countless numbers of churches across the Western world are experiencing decline. In the majority of these cases, churches continue to wrap the unchanging Gospel message in a package that once spoke to a society that is now a distant memory. We continue to "do" things exactly the same way as they were done fifty years ago. In spite of the evident proof of our failure to connect with the culture around us, we continue to maintain the status quo, insanely doing the same things over and over again while expecting different results.

The Church is missionary by her very nature. Parishes are meant to be outposts of the Great Commission. However, most parishes continue to function as self-referential clubs whose primary mission is to serve their own dwindling numbers. A parish becoming missional is something that does not just happen. This transition will only take place if parish leadership is intentional about what they do and how they do it. Good leadership moves a parish toward health, and healthy things grow and bear fruit. As Saint Thomas Aquinas told us, "Grace builds on nature." Being more spiritual is not enough for the renewal of the Church, though it is necessary and desirable. Grace builds on nature; it does not replace it. When a parish is led to a place of health and the people of that parish are open to the Lord and the power of the Holy Spirit, fasten your seat belts because God will work powerfully.

I have been privileged to work closely with Fr. Simon Lobo for over two years, and it has been a joy to see him grow as a result of the investment of so many of the Saint Benedict Parish team members. Of course, we did have some pretty good raw material to work with, but no matter the leadership qualities of any priest, every priest has the capacity to be a better leader if he is open, humble, and willing to work hard. Fr. Simon has been all of these.

I know that you are going to greatly enjoy the reflections in this book. When Simon began his internship experience with us at Saint Benedict Parish, we spoke about having him write a weekly reflection on what he was learning. This would allow him to process and reflect on his experience in the parish and also on the books he was reading and the podcasts he was listening to. It also served as an update to members of his religious community on his internship experience. It was only later that we realized it would make for a great book.

This book represents the third publication within the "Divine Renovation" world. I consider this book to be the third leg of a stool. The original book was a theological and pastoral proposal. The *Divine Renovation Guidebook* was a "how-to" manual, and this third book is a look under the hood of a parish that seeks to be intentional about being missionary. Ultimately, it is the third leg of the stool because it was not written by me!

As I write this foreword, an unexpected development has made the publication of this book more significant. Through a grace-filled intervention, the discernment and call of my bishop, and the discernment of Fr. Simon and his community, the Companions of the Cross, I have stepped aside as pastor of Saint Benedict Parish and joyfully passed the baton of leadership to Fr. Simon. I am now working half-time with the Divine Renovation ministry and half-time supporting the leadership of my bishop and the priests of my diocese, helping them answer the call to move our parishes toward mission.

This brings to full circle an experience I had in the winter of 1993 when, during a break from seminary studies, I found myself in Saint Mary's Parish in Ottawa and encountered Fr. Bob Bedard, the founder of the Companions of the Cross.

What I experienced that weekend confirmed my passion and dream to see parishes fully alive and engaged intentionally in the mission of Jesus Christ: to make disciples of all nations. That weekend I knew that it was indeed possible. I saw it with my very eyes. Years later, when I first met Fr. Simon, we realized that he would have been an eleven-year-old boy actively involved in that very same parish. Who knows, perhaps he was in the sanctuary serving at the altar that weekend.

I pray that all of you who have picked up this book may be inspired by what lies within and that you may transfer this inspiration into action, no matter what your role and ministry within your church. Through your encounter with these reflections may you become a medium for the very message within.

I Am a Catholic Priest

Saint Maximilian Kolbe spoke these words at Auschwitz as he offered his life in place of another: "I am a Catholic priest." The vast majority of priests I know give generously of themselves to serve God and to bless others. I, too, am a Catholic priest (though considerably less heroic than Saint Max). As I am living my priesthood some seventy-five years later, I have recognized that becoming a pastor of a parish is almost inevitable—and that it demands a different kind of self-offering.

With this in mind, I considered myself very privileged as I began a new and unique assignment in July 2015 at Saint Benedict Parish in Halifax, Nova Scotia. I belong to a religious community called the Companions of the Cross, founded in Ottawa, Ontario, in 1985; our primary mission is evangelization. We happen to be closely aligned with Fr. James Mallon, the former pastor of Saint Benedict Parish, and share the same desire to see the Church come alive as individual parishes are renewed.

Before moving to Halifax, I had a chance to chat with a couple from Saint Maurice in Ottawa, my first parish after I was ordained in 2009. I described to them my excitement at being part of this new experiment between the Companions of the Cross and Fr. James' model of Divine Renovation. How many young priests get the chance to be mentored in parish renewal and leadership by a pastor who is doing this work and at a place where it is actually happening? The husband, John, a successful businessman, asked if we had given any thought to how my religious community could gain from this experience.

A week after arriving, I was trying to find my feet in Halifax when, as if in answer to John's questions, both Fr. James and my superior at the Companions of the Cross suggested that I share what I am learning with the community and with the broader Church. So I decided to send out a weekly e-mail with a brief reflection. Right away, several insights came to me that I wanted to take note of before I forgot. If nothing else, these reflections would serve as a record for me of all that I learned, but I hoped others would find them inspiring, practical, and applicable. These reflections have been compiled to form this book.

My aim was to keep my thoughts succinct and clear. Fr. James showed me a simple outline that he created to coach clergy to improve as preachers (see *Divine Renovation Guidebook*, p. 138). It includes a checklist of things that should be in every homily, such as the kerygma (a clear proclamation of the Gospel), something personal (vulnerable), a little humor, and so on. He also asks the preacher to briefly answer three questions to clarify and focus the homily: What do I want people to know? What do I want people to do? Why does it matter? I mention this because his outline is a tool that has been helping me to sharpen and improve as a communicator. In this book, I will end each reflection with a summary of my main point. I also include suggested action items for priests and the lay leaders who support them.

What do I want you to know?

The vocation of priesthood is both wonderful and challenging. I am grateful for all the lay people who serve alongside their priests, not to usurp their role, but to help them to become better leaders. With just over six years of priestly experience (at this writing), I suspect that many readers know more about parish leadership than I do.

In humility, I offer you a year's worth of my reflections based on my insider perspective of Saint Benedict Parish, Fr. James Mallon, and the Divine Renovation model. I have organized these reflections around three major themes that emerged during this year: Transforming Culture, Creating a Game Plan, and Leadership Development. These themes have been integral to the fruit we see at Saint Benedict Parish, and they represent the major areas of learning that I experienced during the first year of my internship.

What do I want you to do?

While anyone is welcome to read along, this book falls under the umbrella of *Divine Renovation*. I am presuming that you have read that groundbreaking book. You can also learn many of the key principles of *Divine Renovation* by watching five video interviews between Peter Herbeck and Fr. James Mallon (see the Resources section).

As you read, you may wish to regularly flip back to the Resources section. I suggest other books, websites, online videos, and a few fun treats to supplement the major themes.

Finally, these reflections are not designed for priests alone, nor for lay people alone, but for teams. If you are a priest, I recommend that you find a few trusted lay leaders, who may or may not be staff, to read along with you. If you are a layperson, you could buy your pastor a copy and encourage him to read it with you. Feel free to read it as fast or as slowly as you wish, but I suggest that you pace yourself. You will learn even more from your team discussions as you try to unpack and apply these reflections in your own context.

Transforming Culture

We most often use the word *culture* in relation to groups of people who share the same ethnicity. In this usage, the culture of an ethnic group relates to things like the food they eat, the music they produce, and the literature they create. It can also refer to the values they hold in common. When we talk about transforming the culture of a parish, we mean something both broader and more precise. A culture in this context represents the assumptions that a group of people makes together (often unconsciously) that shape their behavior and how they see the world around them. Culture, therefore, becomes the environment in which ideas, strategies, and activities are analyzed, evaluated, celebrated, and, possibly, rejected.

In a very real sense, the culture of a parish is the foundational force behind the success of renewal efforts. If a parish culture is not imbued with a missionary emphasis, or if it supports unhealthy behaviors, it will render even the best resources and finest strategies inert. The key to parish transformation lies in the transformation of its culture. The following reflections focus on the ways in which we have tried to shape and transform the culture at Saint Benedict.

CHAPTER 1

Culture Shock

While I was living in Detroit, I made it out to a couple of NHL hockey games at the old Joe Louis Arena (affectionately known as "The Joe"). The late founder of the Companions of the Cross, Fr. Bob Bedard, cheered for the Ottawa Senators as a boy in the 1930s and again when they made a comeback in the 1990s. I share his loyalties. Still, having the chance to see the Red Wings play on home ice was awesome. It was probably some of the best live hockey I will ever get to watch. The fans made it known that "Detroit is Hockeytown!" The atmosphere of that arena spoke volumes about the enthusiasm and the inner convictions of everyone present. It made you want to be a part of it.

Fr. James has spoken and written about the powerful impact of culture. He has often used the analogy of an iceberg. We are aware of the 10 percent above the surface (what we write down and profess to be our cultural values), but it is the 90 percent that is hidden below the water that is the most dangerous—the unspoken and, sometimes, unconscious beliefs and expectations that are lived out as an organization. I recently watched a talk by Bill Hybels, an evangelical pastor from Chicago and a world-renowned leader, in which he spoke about the role of culture within a team. Similarly, the first few pages of Fr. Michael White and Tom Corcoran's book *Rebuilt: The Story of a Catholic Parish* (which I would recommend to priests and lay leaders) mention the primacy of culture.

For the first five years, before I arrived at Saint Benedict, the team had been engaged in a culture war. So many things that are taken for granted in a Catholic parish are unhealthy and keep the focus on maintenance. We tend to do what we are familiar with and what will feed us, the folks who are already members of "the parish club." This is an inevitable death sentence. For example, it's not normal for Catholics to invite friends, family, and the unchurched to their parish. But why not?

A few years ago, the parish staff had a major revelation when they discovered that Alpha—a series of sessions exploring the Christian faith and a tool for evangelization—is not just a good course to run once or twice a year. Alpha is a culture! It is a way of being Church that can change what is below the surface. When used properly, Alpha can influence several areas of parish life: hospitality, fellowship, service, invitation, evangelization, discipleship, leadership, prayer, reading Scripture, growing in spiritual gifts, worship, and more. You will find more on Alpha in chapters 24 and 25 in this book.

When it comes to changing parish culture, a first, manageable step might involve creating a genuinely warm and hospitable environment. I love displaying an image of Clint Eastwood playing one of his gruff characters as an example of what the typical church usher looks like. At Saint Benedict, our hospitality ministry consists of dozens of joyful women and men who simply smile and shake a person's hand as he or she enters church—maybe for the first time.

During my first week when I served as chaplain at Wayne State University, I remember walking into the lounge at lunchtime and seeing a fourth-year student (the old guard) and a brand-new student sitting with their backs to each other. I went over and instinctively welcomed the new person and introduced her to the other student—they had not spoken until that point. It seemed so obvious to me that a Catholic chaplaincy should have a warm atmosphere where people can seek refuge and be known personally. I took it for granted that the more mature members would share this cultural value and know how to be hospitable.

What do I want you to know?

In the words of management consultant Peter Drucker, "Culture eats strategy for breakfast." You can come up with the greatest plans in the world, but if you do not address the unconscious and unhealthy attitudes and behaviors that exist in most Catholic parishes, very little change will occur. Keep in mind that culture is formed by what we reward and what we tolerate.

As in my experience at the Red Wings game, imagine if we could create a Church culture and an atmosphere that would cause even outsiders to say, "That was awesome. I want to be part of that."

What do I want you to do?

Come up with a list of some of the things that you and your parishioners take for granted. Plan one small cultural change. For starters, I would recommend something around welcome and hospitality.

Do not be surprised if parishioners need the priest and lay leaders to model a radical kind of hospitality in a Catholic context. For example, most Sunday mornings Fr. James and Ron Huntley, our former Director of Pastoral Ministries (he is now the lead coach in the Divine Renovation Network), would stand outside greeting people as they arrived for Mass. This is a warm first encounter for people as they walk in. It also sets a great example for the hospitality team.

CHAPTER 2

Uncultured Clerics (Part 1 of 2)

Catholic culture has a kind of gravitational pull that tends to draw everything back toward maintenance mode—that which is more familiar and easier. Fr. James writes at length in *Divine Renovation* about the damaging impact of clericalism, which I believe is among the biggest cultural challenges that face priests today. We are trying to minister in a brave new world under a set of expectations from the good old days. These unrealistic expectations can come from others, but priests can also place them on themselves.

The problem is that Catholics love their priests. The cultural belief is that the priest needs to be at the center of everything remotely connected to parish life, from choosing who gets awarded the snow-removal contract to vetting the Children's Sunday Liturgy weekly craft. If Father does not announce a particular ministry or event, then no one will pay attention to it. What do you mean, Father is not available to attend the Knights of Columbus Treasurer's Year-End Report? One of my brothers in Houston, Fr. Michael Minifie, shared that many of his parishioners (who are professionals) step into his church and instantly become like children, unable to do anything on their own without Father. In every parish, there are also some who are socially awkward or mentally ill and in great need of care and sensitivity as God's children. They can fill up our already busy schedules and drain our reserves.

Fr. James is convinced that there has to be a different way for us to live out our priesthood. Of course, priests are the only ones who can preside at the Eucharist and most other sacraments, and preaching the Word of God should always remain a high priority for us. I feel blessed that my own religious community takes these responsibilities seriously. What is often forgotten is that leadership is the third essential aspect of priestly ministry. Starting with our baptism and reinforced at ordination, we have been anointed priest, prophet, king (or pupil, in my case). The rest of the stuff we do as priests has somehow slipped into our job description.

Running the chaplaincy in Detroit, with virtually no other staff to help me, was a very blessed and very busy time. Ministry of presence was a priority, so I made a point of drinking coffee and playing Ping-Pong with the students. I presided at Mass, which included setting up beforehand and selecting readers daily. I had to manage a couple of e-mail accounts, send out a weekly e-bulletin, and update the Facebook page, not to mention look after all the other administrative tasks associated with scheduling and launching faith study groups. I ran eight of these small groups myself for the first couple of semesters, while overseeing several others. People would drop in to my office to chat, or for the Sacrament of Reconciliation, and I was seeing way too many people for spiritual direction. Just about everyone had my personal cell number, so I was responding to texts day and night. In my spare time, I played soccer on our Catholic intramural team (no thanks to me, but we did win first place that year). In essence, I was trying to do all of the administration, spearhead a new missionary approach, facilitate faith formation, be personable and present, plan strategically, and form the next generation of leaders—all at the same time. But isn't that what a good priest is supposed to do?

What do I want you to know?

One of my brothers in Detroit, Fr. Sean Wenger, suggested that I was the bottleneck at the chaplaincy. It was hard for me to receive this at the time, but he was right. The ministry had the potential to keep growing larger and to have a greater impact on the secular campus, but I was slowing down that progress because everything had to pass through me.

If we try to live according to an old cultural model of priesthood, we will eventually hit a glass ceiling and limit the growth of our parishes. And we will run ourselves off our feet responding to needs in a way that is unsustainable and unhealthy.

What do I want you to do?

If you are a priest, list some of the things you do on a regular basis that are not directly connected with the call to be priest, prophet, and king (to sanctify, to teach, and to govern). Choose one of these items and plan how you will empower someone else to take it over.

If you are a layperson, look at your own expertise and that of the other lay people in the parish. What could you offer to remove from the pastor's plate to free him up to do the things only a priest can do? Make it clear that your motive is not to take away control but to lovingly support him.

CHAPTER 3

Uncultured Clerics (Part 2 of 2)

We need to challenge the priest-centric culture in our churches because it is limiting our ability to form missionary disciples. Early on, I presented the following statistics in a homily at Saint Benedict to drive home this point. In 1970, there were about 650 million Catholics worldwide and just over 400,000 priests. Today there are over 1.2 billion Catholics (approximately double), and still just over 400,000 priests to shepherd them. Furthermore, we need to do more than just take care of the 1.2 billion.

The founder of my community, Fr. Bob Bedard, wrote about this in his first book, *We Are Called to Be Companions of the Cross*: "We are satisfied with a pastoral strategy that is limited to providing religious services to support people on their way to heaven" (p. 14). Most of what we do in our parishes is about servicing the committed believers—about 6 or 7 percent in our congregations. That figure comes from Matthew Kelly's book *The Four Signs of a Dynamic Catholic* and refers to the tiny percentage of Catholics who make up 80 percent of the service and financial giving in a typical parish. As well, a big part of our job is to engage the "sacramentalized and un-evangelized" who are sitting in the pews on Sunday. But the mission of Jesus Christ is to reach *all* seven billion people on the planet! If every last thing needs to go through Father, this will remain a mission impossible.

After high school, I left Ottawa to study life sciences in Kingston, Ontario, with the intention of pursuing medicine. As

I sensed the call to priesthood during my first year of university, I soon became a Queen's University dropout. It had been my desire to be the kind of doctor who did not merely understand the science but one who was able to relate personally to his patients. During my years in seminary, I naturally shifted that mindset, seeing myself as one day becoming a doctor of souls (a personal chaplain), caring for the individuals Christ would entrust to me. This may very well be a common sentiment among priests today.

But given the numbers I mentioned above, priests can no longer spend the majority of their time caring for parishioners one-on-one. We are going to have to let go of a lot of frontline ministries. We will not be available to make every visit to the hospital or nursing home. We will not be free for every dinner invitation. We will not be able to meet individually with every family who approaches the parish seeking the sacraments or a funeral. But if, as Pope Francis says, the Church is to be a field hospital, we cannot leave all of the wounded unattended. We will need to effectively call lay people into leadership positions, so they can in turn lead teams of parishioners. Equipped lay people can go out to the schools and hospitals and be a welcoming presence for all of those knocking on our doors.

As I ponder this, I have been struggling with the fact that I will have to let go of the family-doctor image of priesthood and embrace more of a CEO approach. No one in my immediate family has experience in big business, so these organizational leadership concepts are a little intimidating. What is holding me back is that I get a lot of satisfaction from being engaged in frontline ministry. But when did serving God and others become about me and fulfilling my needs?

What do I want you to know?

Another brother priest in Houston, Fr. Mark Goring, is the director of a Catholic megachurch. (Everything is bigger in Texas.) I recently asked him if he missed doing certain kinds of ministry now that he has to oversee a huge center with a sizeable staff. He told me that he has had to reenvision himself as a military general who, for the greater good, is unable to fight in every skirmish. He has been charged with advancing the kingdom of God by empowering the troops.

It is a sacrifice to let go of ministries we enjoy, but as priests, we have a unique role to play if the field hospital is to be as effective as possible at healing people's wounds.

What do I want you to do?

If you, like me, are a priest who gets satisfaction from doing frontline ministry such as spiritual direction, teaching Bible studies, being present to others, and so forth, I encourage you to make a total surrender of yourself to God in prayer. You might pray something like the following:

> Jesus, I am willing to serve you and your people in the way that I am most needed. I let go of my past successes and failures. Give me a new vision for how to live my priesthood.

For lay leaders, please pray like mad for your priests. This is an extremely difficult transition for a priest. Most of us have been hardwired to help people. It is tough at first to see how taking a step back from people can have a greater impact on many more people in the long run.

CHAPTER 4

A YES of Apostolic Proportions

In a single week in the spring of 2016, I logged about 3,000 kilometers (roughly 1,800 miles) driving to and from Ottawa to attend the episcopal ordination of a brother Companion, Scott McCaig, the new Bishop for the Military Ordinariate of Canada. During this short visit, Fr. James, who is also a friend of the new bishop, was able to join me for dinner at my parents' house in Ottawa. While browsing through old family photos, he tweeted a picture of me as a teenager in my Sea Cadet uniform—my own secret military past. (Sea Cadets is a national youth program sponsored by the Canadian military.)

Leading up to Bishop Scott's ordination, I went through a series of emotions. What is a bittersweet loss for the Companions is a huge gain for the Church in Canada. The Archbishop of Ottawa quipped to the Papal Nuncio that he had better hold off on naming any more Companions of the Cross as bishops for a while (this was our second in two years!). As I have pondered the situation, I have been plagued by this question "Who in their right mind would want to become a bishop today?" In ages gone by, some perks came with the job, whereas now it just seems like an added burden of responsibility. I have tried to picture what it had been like for Fr. Scott to receive the news from the Nuncio a few weeks before. My understanding is that the announcement is "proclaimed" in such a way that the candidate is expected to say yes. But who could possibly give their *fiat*—their yes—and be at peace with such a future?

As a teenager, around the time I was in Sea Cadets, I heard Fr. Bob Bedard, the Companions' founder, speak over and over again about giving God permission. He also impressed upon me the fact that God has a plan—he has a will for my life—and he wants me to say *yes* to that plan without any reservations. This is true for all vocations, and it is true for our universal calling to holiness and to mission—even though in many sectors, Catholic culture still puts these responsibilities squarely on the shoulders of priests and nuns. Jesus awaits our radical and wholehearted *yes*! This no-holds-barred surrender is a first step toward parish renewal. If we think we can "divinely renovate" according to our plans—consulting God from time to time—our efforts will be mediocre at best.

At the end of the ordination, Bishop Scott addressed all in attendance and those watching on Salt + Light TV. He framed his message beautifully, asserting the primacy of peace, though admitting the need to take up arms at times to protect other values. He shared about his own heritage, noting that many of his family members have served in the military. Having said all of that, he gently and clearly directed our gaze to the eternal perspective. This was my favorite zinger: "What good is temporal peace or military victory if we do not have peace with God?" He was confident in his new identity but managed to remain humble. It became evident that I was listening to a man who was speaking with the authority of an apostle.

Today, in my estimation, very few priests desire the heavy responsibility that comes with serving in the hierarchy of the Church. I even know of several priests who are hesitant to accept the burden of leadership that comes with the role of pastor. How did Bishop Scott accept this office? I can only speculate. If you give God one radical yes, you will be put in situations where you will be asked to say yes again and again. Could you suddenly say no to Jesus when he asks you to take one more step closer to him and to his cross?

As the Companions of the Cross motto states, *Accipimus Crucem* (We Embrace the Cross).

What do I want you to know?

Vocations and ordinations aside, every single believer has an apostolic call on his or her life and ministry. Each one of us is being sent to accomplish great things. Yet cultural Catholicism has emphasized the need to stay in control and just do the minimum. Are you willing to let go of your safe parish plan to embrace God's plan for your parish? Jesus' Great Commission is a magnificent mandate for the Church, but it cannot be accomplished by those who are hedging their bets or only halfhearted. Do not be afraid to take risks in following God. Keep in mind that your time on this rock is short—and that is true even for bishops.

What do I want you to do?

If you have not given your life to Jesus in an absolute fashion, now is the time to do it. I have given God permission in the past, but I often try to take back control. Somehow I think I know what is best for my future. I am willing to do *some* things to build God's kingdom but not *other* things. Witnessing Bishop Scott's ordination has challenged me: I need to renew my total commitment to God and to his plan, wherever that will lead. If you are like me, I urge you to recommit your allegiance to the Lord and go where he takes you.

Fr. James was inspired to lead Saint Benedict with this bold vision in part because he saw it happen in other places, such as at Saint Mary's Parish in Ottawa. God used Fr. Bob Bedard to bring about great transformation there, and it all started with a simple inspiration that led to what he called the *Dangerous Prayer* (which was published weekly in the bulletin). Feel free to use this prayer personally and at your parish. This is the version that I try to pray:

Jesus, I will do anything you want me to do, and I say YES to that thing even before I know what it is. Amen.

CHAPTER 5

Preaching with Intent

After a weekday Mass when I was working on campus, a student casually said, "You know, Father, I've noticed that you really bring your A game on Sundays." I was not sure if he was affirming me for my Sunday preaching or commenting on the "Random Thoughts from Fr. Simon" that he had just sat through. But people do speak of the high caliber of homilies they have come to expect from Companions of the Cross priests. They appreciate the personal examples, the humor, the clarity, the focus on Jesus, the application to everyday life, and the passion we bring.

Proclaiming the word is a gift from God, but I also work at it a lot. For example, since my ordination, I have been recording my Sunday homilies with an MP3 recorder so I can go back and listen to them. I am not just reviewing the content but listening to my style of delivery—modulation, speed, energy, and so on—so I can improve.

When it comes to communicating on Sundays, the book *Rebuilt* recommends developing a "message series" as opposed to the weekly stand-alone homily. While I was in Detroit, I preached periodically at the parish of Fr. John Riccardo, an innovating pastor in the Archdiocese of Detroit who was also trying to encourage thematic preaching that built from one week to the next. As an example, we did a four-week series on the Four Last Things. As I began to preach one Sunday, I joked about how he insisted that I speak on purgatory (it was either that or hell). But seriously, I think he was on to something.

During that same period, I attempted my own four-week series at the chaplaincy based on Matthew Kelly's book *The Four Signs of a Dynamic Catholic*: prayer, study, generosity, and evangelization.

Just before being assigned to Saint Benedict Parish, I was made administrator at a parish in Ottawa for six months. Since I knew that my time there was short, I laid out a preaching schedule for myself, alternating with another priest. I decided to glance at the readings for the weeks when I would be up to bat. There were a few key topics that I felt were important to cover—most of which fit naturally, at some point or other, with the Lectionary. The community had suffered through some traumatic events before my arrival, so for the first few weeks I tried to affirm them for sticking around and I emphasized God's love. I spoke about prayer right before Lent and encouraged people to use Fr. Mark Goring's forty-day prayer booklet *Treasure in Heaven*. We sold 800 copies! I made sure to give refreshers on Reconciliation and the Eucharist around the time when the children were receiving these sacraments. I picked a weekend to share my story of personal conversion. In my last few weekends—after building a level of trust—I gave more challenging messages about the mission of Jesus and their specific call as laity. In general, I found that mapping out a schedule helped me to prepare clear and inspiring homilies.

All of these experiences prepared me to take preaching to a whole new level as I got settled at Saint Benedict. We met as a Senior Leadership Team to brainstorm a preaching series that Fr. James and I would deliver. Rob McDowell, the Director of Parish Life, who has a lot of preaching experience, navigated through our Lectionary from September to November and found a seven-week period with an overarching theme. He suggested titles and topics for each Sunday. Kate Robinson, our Director of Communications, came up with a branding image and published these topics ahead of time.

Since our goal is to be missional, if parishioners have an idea of what to expect, they can invite friends and family to church on a weekend that might be appealing. Also, for those who attend off and on, they might get hooked and come several weeks in a row. Even our faithful parishioners said how much they enjoyed and remembered the homilies as we stayed with a theme for a few weeks. Repetition is the mother of learning.

What do I want you to know?

Preaching matters! Yet in most Catholic parishes, the bar has been set so low that most homilists would trip over it. The cultural belief is that people expect to be bored on Sundays. When it comes to delivering homilies, every priest can become a better communicator. Creating a long-term preaching schedule and coming up with a few shorter thematic series throughout the year will help make the message stick, as well as reinforce cultural change.

It is incredibly freeing to know that I have a team of people who support my homily preparation for Sundays. Even Fr. James, who is a gifted and experienced communicator, says that his preaching has gone to a new level. I think we push each other to be the best we can be—for the glory of God and the salvation of souls.

What do I want you to do?

Rather than waiting until Friday afternoon for inspiration from the Holy Spirit about the weekend homily, sit down with your brother priests, deacons, and a few lay leaders and have a strategic meeting on preaching. Prayerfully map out what the next couple of months of homilies could look like.

Experiment with a short preaching series that respects the Lectionary and focuses on a particular theme. Be attentive to feedback from the congregation.

CHAPTER 6

Outside In

When I was a teenager, I created a secret handshake with one of my buddies from youth group. From across a crowded room, the two of us would nonchalantly walk toward each other without making eye contact. At the last second, we would turn around (going back-to-back), lean forward, and shake hands between our legs. As I write this, the whole thing sounds quite bizarre. Still, it was fun to see the confused looks from bystanders, many of whom were left scratching their heads. My friends and I also had countless inside jokes that we would repeat to one another whenever we got together. If you are not yet convinced that laughter, humor, and joy are connected to holiness, then I recommend you read *Between Heaven and Mirth* by Fr. James Martin, SJ.

That being said, the weekend homily is not a suitable place for inside jokes. In fact, it is easy for priests to make simple, subtle comments, humorous or otherwise, that will only be understood by the Catholic "insiders." Between Masses one Sunday, Fr. James affirmed me on the message I had given but then pointed out that I had mentioned a person's name in reference to a quote. Only a small percentage of our parishioners—let alone our visitors—would know that this person works at the archdiocesan office. Putting myself in the shoes of an unchurched person sitting in the pew, I realized that they might have been left thinking, "I guess everyone else must know who so-and-so is."

It seems like a minor point, possibly fifteen to twenty seconds in a fifteen-to-twenty-minute homily. But the key principle is important. If listeners who are loosely connected to the parish hear offhand insider comments on a regular basis, they will begin to feel even more disengaged from the community. A simple fix, when mentioning a name or a situation that only a few would recognize, is to add a brief line of explanation: "So-and-so, one of the guys who works for the Archdiocese of Halifax-Yarmouth, once said . . . "

A few days later, Fr. James raised the point again, referring to a second time in that same homily where I left a hanging comment that only a quarter of the parishioners would have understood. Feeling as if he was dissecting my homily, I reacted quickly and defensively. For those who have seen the brilliant Pixar movie *Inside Out*, you will be able to picture the five characters in the young girl's head representing five human emotions: joy, sadness, fear, anger, and disgust. One of them tends to take charge. In my head, anger is the go-to emotion that is usually running the control board. As I walked away from that encounter, disappointed by my response, I questioned if this was my issue (in receiving) or Fr. James' issue (in communicating). My guess is that it was a mixture of both.

Sparks are going to fly, especially when you have two strong personalities, both passionate to see God's Church renewed. A couple of days later, we were able to clear the air and reconcile. One of the things I love about ministering alongside Fr. James is not that we work seamlessly—though we have great rapport—but that we are both committed to unity. The stakes are too high for us to let things fester, which could leave room for the enemy to get between us.

What do I want you to know?

If a priest uses inside jokes or is in the habit of name dropping during the weekend homily, the outsiders will be reinforced in the lie that they do not really belong at the parish. At best, they will feel like second-tier participants.

One of the cultural tendencies for us in *churchworld* is to get comfortable speaking predominantly to *churchpeople* (to use terms from the book *Rebuilt)*. Many of us assume that just about everyone has heard of certain Catholic celebrities. But people's circumstances and backgrounds differ, so why would they?

What do I want you to do?

When a priest is preparing to preach, he needs to consider the listeners who are still on the outside. First, think that for the people there, attending Mass on Sundays is the exclusive manifestation of their faith. They will be oblivious to other parish activities, small groups, or diocesan events. Second, think about the people who make it to Mass once or twice a month. If you are attempting a preaching series, building week by week, try not to leave these people behind, even though they might have missed a week. Last but not least, be sensitive to the guests who might be at church for the first time. How will your comments help to draw them in?

A secondary challenge would be for priests to seek honest feedback on their homilies from lay people who are able to listen with the ears of an unchurched person. One of my blind spots is that I unconsciously presume that I am speaking only to Catholic disciples. It has been humbling to learn about my blind spots, but I would rather this than be blindsided—discovering that I have said or done something to push a person away.

I distinctly remember a prophetic word that Fr. Bob Bedard shared at one of our Companions of the Cross gatherings some years ago: "The Lord says, humble yourself . . . or get humbled!"

CHAPTER 7

Microphone Check

Last year I attended the Archbishop's annual fundraising dinner, which was actually a lot of fun. An impressive master of ceremonies and a charming auctioneer kept us entertained. Both were hilarious and were able to get the job done. I was amazed at the way the auctioneer seemed to have a personal connection with several people in the crowd. He had a lighthearted way of encouraging us to be generous. The only other smooth-operating auctioneer I know of who can work a crowd with ease is my brother Companion Fr. Jim Lowe (he used to be a DJ, but that's another story).

Lately, I have been reflecting on the fact that a good MC can have a powerful impact on setting the tone for a gathering. After some prodding from Ron Huntley, our former Director of Pastoral Ministries, I agreed to be the MC for our Friday evening Alpha. Thankfully, a layman from the parish gave me his thorough notes after serving in this role the previous year. Alpha is meant to be a fun, hospitable place (similar to a dinner party) where people can explore together the most important questions in life. The formula demands that the MC start each evening with an overused lame joke—my least favorite part. Still, I know how to embellish a good story and found a way to make a fool of myself week after week. I considered it a win even if the guests were laughing *at* me.

In addition to helping strangers relax in an unfamiliar environment, the MC is also responsible for offering direction and vision. Over the first few weeks, I tried to remind people to be sensitive to the fact that we all come from different backgrounds: some were non-Catholics, and some were not religious at all. Assume nothing about your fellow tablemates! This is one of those leaky cultural elements that people need to be reminded of again and again.

Later, I also found myself serving as moderator (or MC) at an evening of praise and worship for almost two hundred parishioners and guests. Again, I got up in front of the crowd, tried to set people at ease with a few funnies, got people moving around, and then challenged them to take worship to the next level. I taught the crowd step-by-step how to use hand gestures and enter into spontaneous praise—something I had done while working with students on campus in Detroit. After singing the lyrics of a praise song, I invited those attending the praise and worship evening to sing freely from their hearts to God's heart. All these exercises stretched people out of their comfort zones. Yet with a bit of humor and clear direction at the outset, the praise that night was incredible.

For the sake of my own humility, I should also share a "fail" that occurred at our first RCIA orientation session that year. (The Rite of Christian Initiation of Adults is the program through which adults interested in becoming Catholic join the Church.) About fifteen of us, including the RCIA team, gathered on a Sunday afternoon to talk about the process of becoming Catholic at Saint Benedict. I was running around making photocopies at the last minute, so from the start there was confusion about the snack table, filling out forms, and so on. I finally gathered our little group to say a quick word of welcome, but I had set things up so that they sat in rows of chairs, lecture-style. Given the size of our group, it would have made more sense to seat

CHAPTER 8

Making a List, Checking It Twice

Every time our southern neighbours (and, yes, I spell it with a *u*) gather for American Thanksgiving—the tricelebration of family, food, and football—I am reminded of the materialistic mayhem that will ensue from Black Friday to Cyber Monday. Many people use these days—and the must-have door-crashing deals—as an opportunity to check a few major items off their Christmas shopping lists. This, naturally, would free up a person to enter into the season of Advent with an unhindered devotion to prayer, silence, and minor acts of mortification. Right?

Inflatable nativity scenes aside, and other such things that prepare the soul for the Solemnity of the Incarnation, what kind of a checklist should a pastor have when he arrives at a new parish?

Years ago, when I was in seminary formation, a Companion priest, Fr. Jim MacGillivray, wisely cautioned us not to get too excited about the first few people who approach the new pastor as he begins at his parish. Some of the real gems in that parish will sit back for a little while, trying to figure out if you (Father) are trustworthy. Similarly, the pastor must begin by observing his people. This takes patience. You will not be able to figure everyone out after the first week or the first month.

In one of our early meetings, Fr. James Mallon's practical advice to me was to start by making a list of the people in the parish who appear to have a degree of influence. This does not necessarily refer to the ones who are involved in a number of ministries or the ones who pray the most or give the most, though it could.

Leadership is all about influence. Who are the parishioners who seem to have others following them? It could be one of the higher-ups in the Knights of Columbus or the Catholic Women's League (or the equivalent in your country). It could be a long-serving usher or a choir member or someone who runs the kitchen. It could be someone involved in a ministry that you might not consider essential to parish renewal. Very likely, some of the people on this list will have difficult personalities or might differ from your own theological leanings and your pastoral priorities. Yet these individuals wield influence.

Fr. James suggests that a new pastor needs to make time for the people on this list. Set up a meeting with them or invite them out for coffee—in most cases, one at a time. Love them and listen to them. Try to understand their history with the parish. As the expression goes, you might even want to burn a little incense at the altar of whatever they consider to be sacred. In the early phase of a parish assignment, if you identify the people of influence and take the time to win them over, it will pay dividends later on. In time, many will warm up to your leadership. For everyone else, there is leftover turkey and apple pie.

What do I want you to know?

Real people, with real histories, have really cared about their parish long before any pastor has arrived and long after he will depart. And because of the time and energy that some of these people have poured into their parish, they have earned the trust and respect of their fellow parishioners—whether or not they are influencing them in a positive direction. Strategically winning over several of these leaders will help you to move the culture of the parish community toward mission.

What do I want you to do?

A priest should try to identify the key players at the parish. Once you have made a list of these influencers, begin to meet with them. Honor them and show them that you genuinely care about them, their past, and their motivations.

If you are a lay leader whom the pastor has already won over, try to meet with some of these other parish influencers to hear them out. Be aware that some of these individuals, because they have absorbed the clerical mindset that has long been part of Catholic life, will only open up if they get face time with the priest.

Refer to the exercise in *Divine Renovation Guidebook*, pp. 18–21.

This might be a good opportunity to review some of Dale Carnegie's timeless advice from *How to Win Friends and Influence People*:

Six Ways to Make People Like You

1. Become genuinely interested in other people. Smile.
2. Remember that a person's name is, to that person, the sweetest and most important sound in any language.
3. Be a good listener. Encourage others to talk about themselves.

4. Talk in terms of the other person's interest.
5. Make the other person feel important—and do it sincerely.*

* Dale Carnegie, *How to Win Friends & Influence People*, rev. ed., (New York: Pocket Books, 1981), p. 112.

CHAPTER 9

Amping Up for Christmas

I f you have not yet seen the *Saturday Night Live* church skit from 2014, you are missing out. Whoever wrote the skit is either a C&E Catholic (that is, Christmas and Easter, or a "Chreaster") or is well aware of this phenomenon. The skit accurately depicts how foreign church would feel for a person who goes only once or twice a year. It manages to capture the experience of listening to a disinterested, mumbling teenage reader, followed by a militant, overly keen "proclaimer" of the Word of God. The priest tells a lame joke in his homily, which receives a lame laugh. The choir belts out every single verse of *O Come All Ye Faithful*, including the Latin ("Is this song still about Jesus?"). The sad truth is that Catholic liturgies are notorious for not only being boring but creating an atmosphere that is confusing and unwelcoming to outsiders.

In 2015 our Senior Leadership Team developed a plan to prepare the parish intentionally for the deluge of visitors on December 24 and 25. First, Rob McDowell, our Director of Parish Life, helped us create a four-week preaching series, synchronized with the four Sundays of Advent, titled "Getting Ready for Company." I recall a brother Companion, Fr. Sean Wenger, launching a similar endeavor in the Archdiocese of Detroit under the title *Who's Sitting in My Pew?* Fr. James and I used the analogy of having houseguests, whether for dinner or overnight, as a way to communicate the disposition and preparation needed to make our visitors feel welcome.

We also challenged parishioners to invite their family and friends to our parish at Christmas, and we gave them simple ideas for how to do it. Concretely, we asked our regular parishioners to up the ante on hospitality (be warm and smiling, for example), to park across the street at the mall (our parking lot is grossly inadequate even on a regular Sunday), and, at the busiest Mass—7:30 p.m. on December 24—to opt to sit in the church basement, where the Mass would be shown on Livestream. We wanted to leave the best seats for our visitors. Parishioners who were bringing guests, however, were encouraged to sit in the church with them.

Over the four weeks, there was some repetition in our preaching. Apparently, a message needs to be heard at least seven times before it really starts to sink in. Apparently, a message needs to be heard at least seven times . . . (just kidding). As you can imagine, there was some pushback with regard to these various "asks." Building a culture of invitation and welcome at any parish is hard work.

Besides offering radical hospitality at the Masses, we came up with the idea of having a nonliturgical Christmas service in the basement at 4 p.m. on December 24. We called it *Christmas Unplugged*. It is designed as one of those shallow-water entry points that would be ideal for a non-Catholic or lapsed Catholic. In other words, we wanted to make it as easy as possible for our parishioners to invite a friend or family member. Rather than forcing these people to sit through a long liturgy—with a lot of standing and kneeling and unfamiliar responses—we wanted to bring them to a kid-friendly environment with great people, top-quality music, and a down-to-earth message.

Given Rob's past experience speaking to the unchurched, he seemed best suited to preach during the one-hour Christmas service. Meanwhile, Fr. James and the staff were present to greet our guests.

What do I want you to know?

Everyone knows that tons of people who do not normally go to church show up at our parishes at Christmastime. Some might have grown up practicing their faith but now go to church only a couple times a year. Others are visiting family from out of town and may or may not attend church at home. Still others have never really had a strong connection to church and yet feel compelled to show up.

This is a huge opportunity to reach the lost. We don't even need to go looking for them, because many of them are willing to come to us at this time of year if we issue a simple invitation. We need to begin by creating a space for belonging.

What do I want you to do?

Pray for your parish (and all parishes) that they would strive to be warm and hospitable. Pray also for all the people who will be walking through your doors at Christmastime.

Start to think about the next time the nonregulars show up *en masse* for Mass, such as Ash Wednesday, the Good Friday liturgy, Easter Sunday, weddings, funerals, and the sacraments of initiation. Think of how you can intentionally prepare to receive these non-churchgoers as welcome guests. What do you need to do to prepare regular parishioners to be welcoming? When you have the visitors captive for that brief window of time, how will you invite them to take a next step? We invited our guests to our next six-week preaching series, "A Place for Everyone," starting on Epiphany Sunday. And as always, we invited everyone to Alpha.

CHAPTER 10

Pointers for Pastoral Presiding

I n the previous chapter, I wrote about the Christmas of 2015 when we prepared very intentionally for our guests. That year we had five celebrations and well over 3,000 people came through the building. The celebrations included our nonliturgical Christmas Unplugged (CUP) service, which had about 120 guests and fifteen staff and volunteers (The second year we offered CUP, the number of guests doubled!). Fr. James dressed up as Saint Nick at CUP and read a children's Christmas story. Unfortunately, he had a wardrobe malfunction with his beard and was exposed by one of the girls as a "fake Santa."

All in all, the efforts of our Advent four-week preaching series "Getting Ready for Company" were well received. Here are a few other things we incorporated at our Christmas Masses. Before each of the Masses, we had one or two staff members give a welcome message, followed by a short video to set the tone for Christmas Mass. We also put *Why Jesus?* booklets (an Alpha resource) in the pews. Many people flipped through them as they waited for Mass to begin. We invited our guests to take a copy home with them. As with any liturgy where a lot of nonpracticing folks are present, Fr. James added a few explanations to give guidance at key moments. Here are a few paraphrases of the main messages:

Greeting (before the Penitential Rite): "We have a local custom at Saint Benedict—we want everyone to have a 'prayer partner.' Don't worry; it's not difficult. It helps us to enter into Mass as a community together. We want to make sure that each person here has someone else praying for him or her. Turn to a person near you, introduce yourself, and agree to pray for them. Later, at the end of the Prayers of the Faithful, we will have an opportunity to offer a silent prayer, in our hearts, for that person."

Sign of Peace: "As we are about to offer one another a sign of peace, let's remember that this gesture is, in a sense, a prayer. 'I pray that you know peace in your life,' the kind of peace that Jesus brings to us in a special way at Christmastime."

Communion: "For the sake of visitors from outside our tradition: in a few moments we will have distribution of Holy Communion. It represents union with Jesus, but it is also *a public declaration of being an active member of the Catholic Church.* We want to respect everyone, and we don't want anyone to make that kind of statement if it is not true. We want you to be true to yourself. If you are in a place where you are not able to receive Holy Communion, you are welcome to come forward. We simply ask that you cross your arms over your chest, and we will be happy to pray a blessing over you."

(I was shocked to see the number of people who came forward with arms crossed and with smiles on their faces. I think they felt free to not have to pretend.)

Leaving Early (could be added to the pre-Communion announcement): "This is a very special time of prayer. Please don't leave. It's not over until it's over. We've still got some praying to do. We'll get home—the turkey is still half-frozen, the gifts are still going to be there. Just stay and be with Jesus, and let's take a moment of prayer together."

(I was amazed by how few "Judases" we had—people who leave the supper early.)

What do I want you to know?

At Saint Benedict, we presume that there will be guests in our midst all the time, but especially at Christmas. As a result, we went out of our way to make the typical outsider-unfriendly liturgy as warm and understandable as possible.

In the past, I have often been annoyed with unchurched people who do not know what to say or do at Mass. It has been a good exercise for me to look inward and ask, "What am I doing to set our guests up for success?" The fruit is that many commented on how they felt welcome, and some said that they planned to come back.

What do I want you to do?

Discuss with your liturgy team which of these messages and tactics would be appropriate in your own situation. Be attentive to the high-traffic seasons when you anticipate having a lot of people who are unfamiliar with the Mass. Consider using one of these guest-sensitive instructions during Mass at the next available opportunity and then evaluate how it goes.

Every priest has his own presidential style and take on liturgy. I'm not suggesting that this is *the* way to go or that implementing a few of these ideas will save the day. They are part of a much broader approach—to create an "invitational culture" that is welcoming to outsiders.

CHAPTER 11

The Giver

Awhile ago, I went to visit a family for dinner. Their youngest daughter, with a group of siblings and friends, greeted me at the end of the driveway. They were selling homemade bracelets and giving the proceeds to the local hospital. In response to the winning smile and the incredible confidence of that nine-year-old, I found myself pulling a $5 bill out of my wallet. I made a mental note to see if there was an opening on our Stewardship of Treasure Committee at the parish. That young lady has a knack for calling forth the gift of generosity in people.

We had just completed a three-week preaching series on giving titled "Living for Eternity." Over the past few years, this has become an annual and recurring message. Initially, many people were offended that Fr. James would dare to speak about money in such a sacred place. However, since Jesus spoke frequently about money in the Gospels, we believe this should be a topic discussed at the parish on a regular basis. In principle, Fr. James makes the distinction between "fundraising" and "raising givers." We are interested primarily in the latter.

One of our intern priests, Fr. Michael Leclerc from Montreal, told me how his parish responded to the global refugee crisis. One Sunday he made a "soft ask," explaining that it was important for his parishioners to support their brothers and sisters in need. Their little parish received contributions of about $18,000 over a couple of weekends. Months later, two Montreal parishes joined forces to plan a fundraising concert for refugees. The underlying assumption went something like this: "I will not give generously to help families in war-torn situations who have been forced to flee from their homes . . . *unless* you entertain me first." After all the effort and expense of hosting the concert, they raised only $13,000 (about a third of the $18,000 mentioned above, if you divide it between the two parishes).

Granted, if community building is one of your objectives, there is a time and a place for parish concerts and dinners. One year the Saint Benedict youth group made an appeal to help offset the cost of sending a group of teens to the Steubenville Atlantic youth conference. A few weeks later, they invited the parish to a pancake breakfast after the Masses to say thank you. Though some people continued to contribute at the breakfast, the teens served syrup-laden flapjacks primarily as a sign of gratitude.

On the final week of our preaching series, Fr. James invited parishioners to commit to giving by filling out a card placed in the pews. Instead of one broad appeal, he spoke of degrees of giving. For those who had not been giving (including teens with jobs), he asked them to commit to start giving. Ron Huntley, our former Director of Pastoral Ministries, loves to quote (now retired) Bishop Robert Morneau of Green Bay, Wisconsin, who said, "If you can't give a dime out of a dollar, you'll never be able to give $100 out of $1,000." Others who gave sporadically were asked to give regularly. Those who gave regularly were encouraged to give through automatic withdrawal. Still others were exhorted to become generous or even extravagant givers. Music played as parishioners filled out the cards. When they were ready, they "stepped up" and dropped their cards in a basket placed in front of the altar.

What do I want you to know?

If our parishes are going to fulfill the mission of Jesus Christ, we are going to need money to get the job done. The best way to get that money is not only to raise the funds but to find creative ways to raise the givers.

Fr. Bob Bedard had a freedom around money in his personal life. He did not live in abject poverty, nor did his life smack of luxuries and excess. He lived simply, was very generous with others and the Church, and was detached from his earthly possessions. When it came to the mission, he quoted Haggai 2:8 with radical trust and confidence: "The silver is mine, and the gold is mine, says the Lord of hosts."

What do I want you to do?

Most of us find it hard to ask for money. One time I was at a BMW dealership, accompanying a potential buyer. The person I was with suggested that the cost of the car was inflated because there was a BMW sticker on the hood. The salesman, trained to respond to the standard objections, did not bat an eye nor did he apologize for the price. He simply said that with the emblem comes the quality that BMW drivers have come to expect. The salesman knew the value of what he was selling. Guess who went home that day with a sizeable commission?

Church leaders need to overcome their awkwardness when it comes to speaking about money, especially since we are offering Jesus—the pearl of great price. Reflect on your own personal relationship with money. Where do you need more freedom and detachment? Reflect also on your assumptions when asking for money. For example:

- They will think I'm being greedy or I'm asking too much.
- They will think I'm insensitive and don't know what it's like to raise a family.
- They will think the Church is too focused on money, control, and power.

Bring your discomfort to Jesus, and ask him to give you confidence and joy, like that of the little girl in the family I visited for dinner. We need to be able to close the deal and get on with the mission!

See the Saint Benedict website in the Resources section for fresh ideas to promote giving.

CHAPTER 12

To Die For

Fr. Bernie O'Neill—the pastor who brought together three church communities and built Saint Benedict—assembled an amazing funeral ministry before Fr. James became the pastor. This team of lay volunteers handles triage as funeral requests come in. They coordinate with the funeral home and meet with the family to arrange the readings and music and to field questions around eulogies, receptions, bagpipes, and so on. They try to get a sense of the faith life and virtues of the deceased so that notes can be supplied to the presider to help us personalize our homilies. This is a tremendous service to those in the early stages of grieving, and it is also a great blessing to the priests.

Statistics show that fewer and fewer people are receiving the sacraments in the West. The one constant seems to be the steady flow of funerals. These may or may not include a Mass, but they are significant moments on people's faith journeys. There is no question that burying the dead is one of the corporal works of mercy and thus a responsibility that every parish must take seriously. With that said, a pastor leading a 21st-century parish can get "buried" under these unexpected requests that come in the midst of an already busy week.

Sadly, the majority of these funerals are for, and attended by, people who have had little connection to the parish and to God in recent years. Should we continue to offer services in a way that caters to the convenience of these unchurched consumers? When it was suggested that we must be willing to bend over backwards because one of our parish mottos is "All are welcome!" Fr. James brilliantly responded, "Welcome to what?" Every person—no matter what their background—is welcome, and we want to invite them to take a step on a journey of faith that we hope will lead to an encounter with the person of Jesus. On the other hand, we are not saying that "all are welcome" to take advantage of our staff and facilities.

The real question remains: *Is a funeral an effective investment in evangelization?* I hear this kind of comment often: "Five years ago, Fr. X did such a beautiful job celebrating my grandmother's funeral. He was so kind, and his words were so touching." But if you were to ask the person if this has had any tangible impact on their faith life in the last five years, you would most likely find that they are just as disconnected from the parish (and from Jesus) as they were before. As I see it, we have two responsibilities moving forward. We should try to leverage funerals as a point of connection, preaching the Gospel and inviting the unchurched to things like Alpha. And we need to put some boundaries and processes in place so that funerals are not the death of us.

What do I want you to know?

You can't expect a parish to become alive, to be healthy, and to bear fruit if a large percentage of a pastor's week is spent preparing for and burying the dead. It's death by funeral!

I realize that this goes against the fiber of most priests, who have the instinct to do everything they can to help people in need. But I am aware of situations where pastors are expected to celebrate three, four, even five funerals in a single week and sometimes to also lead services at funeral homes. Funeral requests are in high demand, and usually the most demanding people are the ones who are the least interested in belonging to the community and growing in faith. As Jesus said in Luke 9:60, "Leave the dead to bury their own dead; but as for you, go and proclaim the kingdom of God." Those who are spiritually indifferent should not be permitted to monopolize dozens of priest hours. While still performing this important corporal work of mercy, we need to be good stewards of our limited resources. A priest should try to manage expectations, minister with compassion, and then move on.

What do I want you to do?

If you have not yet had the chance, read Fr. Michael White and Tom Corcoran's book *Tools for Rebuilding*. It is filled with short, practical chapters dealing with everyday pastoral situations. Chapter 41, "Funerals Are Scud Missiles," is full of wisdom and is written from the lived experience of a pastor.

Based on my reading and my own experience, here are a few recommendations to consider:

- Train a team of lay volunteers (most likely folks who are retired) to meet with families and funeral directors and to organize the funeral liturgies.

- If it seems as if the deceased and the majority of those who will be attending are unchurched, you could suggest that the family consider a funeral Liturgy of the Word outside of

Mass. This could be led by a deacon or a layperson. Given the efficacious power of the Eucharist, a Mass intention can be offered at a later date for the deceased.

- Decide that funerals can only take place on certain days of the week (for example, Tuesdays, Wednesdays, and Fridays) and almost never on a priest's day off.

- Send someone (again, a deacon or lay funeral team member) to lead prayers at the vigil, and only if the family requests this.

- Ask a deacon or funeral team member to lead the prayers at the gravesite.

(Please note that our local archbishop has given provisions for all of these adaptations.)

Naturally, if the pastor knew the deceased personally, and the person had a deep faith and was an active member of the parish, the pastor may choose to be more involved.

CHAPTER 13

A Little Mess Is Good

r. James caught me sweeping out my office one day and posted a picture of this "sight for sore eyes" on Twitter. The caption read: "It's about time @frsimoncc cleaned up his act." Believe me when I say that I have a lot more cleaning to do. For those of us who are working toward the renewal of the Church, the "mess" that needs to be cleaned up can be daunting. Many would feel more comfortable if everything was tidied up first before we start to move forward. I am reminded of something Fr. Bob Bedard often said: "The work of renewal is messy!"

Pope Francis said something similar when he was addressing the young people of Argentina during World Youth Day in Brazil in 2013. The pope encouraged them, saying, "I hope there will be noise. . . . May the bishops and priests forgive me if some of you create a bit of confusion afterwards. That's my advice. Thanks for whatever you can do" (Address, July 25, 2013).

These reflections around confusion and holy chaos were on my mind as I came across half a dozen "messy" situation at the parish. (For the record, the dust bunnies in my office are the least of my worries.) I encountered most of these messy circumstances through RCIA. Many people who come through this process to become Catholic are divorced and remarried, and others are parents who are yet to be married. A few, I suspect unknowingly, have made ties to practices that are New Age or even borderline occult. Needless to say, there are no quick fixes for any of these complicated scenarios.

Though I'm relatively young, I have done enough parish ministry to feel jaded by all the people who show up on the church doorstep with urgent sacramental demands. Over the years, I have had to contend with one or two bridezillas, a few customized funeral requests, and a handful of emotional parents begging that their kids be confirmed alongside their friends even though the parents missed two out of two parent sessions. In their eyes, the fear of rejection and the inevitable therapy sessions in midlife seem reason enough to give their child a pass. Almost all of these people have had little or no connection to Jesus or his Church. Few show any interest in being around long-term. Most approach the parish seeking a service—or a sacramental milestone—before they continue on with their busy lives.

Yet the half a dozen cases I was dealing with were of a totally different nature. My attitude toward these complicated scenarios that I encountered and continue to encounter is shifting, because all these people are in the Saint Benedict Game Plan, the pastoral strategy that we will discuss in later chapters. All have taken or are taking Alpha, and many are involved in some form of a parish-based group to help them grow in their faith. Every one of them has a relationship with God, feels at home in our parish, and attends Mass weekly. These are wonderful people who are asking for sacraments and demonstrating that they want to be in the discipleship process. So how can we help them clean up their mess?

What do I want you to know?

If we are reaching to the fringes—as Pope Francis is urging us—then we can expect to encounter more and more people who have made a mess of some aspect of their past. If we find ourselves working with these people, it is a sign that we are doing something right!

I have discovered that there are two basic categories of "messy" people. First, there are those who show up with no intention of connecting with the parish or with God but who *demand* the sacraments—often on their own terms. And then there are those who have been evangelized and are already connected to the parish, perhaps through Alpha or a small group. At a certain point in their journey, they begin to hunger for the sacraments. We must be prepared to focus the lion's share of our pastoral energy and resources on this second group.

What do I want you to do?

When it comes to "messy" people, I would suggest that we all need a change of heart. Begin by taking the whole situation to prayer, perhaps by meditating on Luke 15:1-7 (the parable of the lost sheep). May God give us a heart for the lost so that we may continuously seek them out and willingly get the smell of the sheep on us, as Pope Francis would say.

Fr. James Mallon has suggested that most Catholic parishes operate out of a Behave > Believe > Belong paradigm. The attitude toward newcomers sounds something like the following: first you must behave a certain way; then you must believe what we believe; if you fulfill these conditions, you may belong to our tribe. Imagine flipping that culture preconception on its head. The first message is that God loves you and so do we, period. As we develop a trusting relationship, we want to share some of the things that we believe, with the hope that you will embrace these beliefs also. In the end, we desire that true beliefs will lead to a change in your behavior.

If your parish is going to embrace a Belong > Believe > Behave approach, how will that change the way you pastorally welcome and challenge people who show up with their mess?

We have to be willing to walk with people on a step-by-step journey (*Lex Gradualitatis* = Law of Gradualism) without giving in to an approach that disregards objective truth (*Gradualitas Legis* = Gradualism of the Law). The latter suggests that there should be various degrees of law to conform to a variety of persons. What matters most is that we become comfortable ministering in the midst of this uncomfortable tension.

CHAPTER 14

But Who's Counting?

I have to confess that I have watched far too many episodes of the original *A-Team*, often with a fellow fan and brother priest, Fr. Tim Devine. Mr. T's character, B. A. Baracus, was definitely my favorite, but each member of the special-ops unit brought something unique and fun to the group. The show was formulaic, with lots of gunfire and explosions, but since it was on prime-time TV back in the day, no one was ever fatally wounded. In every episode, John "Hannibal" Smith, the leader, with a cigar in hand, would say, "I love it when a plan comes together." So do I.

Take the RCIA program. I beamed like a proud father as twelve adults were baptized and/or received into full communion in the Catholic Church at the Easter Vigil in 2016. (By God's grace, we received twenty people through RCIA at Saint Benedict in 2017.)

Ron Huntley, the former Director of Pastoral Ministries, observed that we make a big deal out of small groups of individuals who first receive the sacraments as adults. Yet there are dozens upon dozens of others who received the sacraments as children but don't really come into a full experience and acceptance of their faith until they are adults. Some have returned to weekly Sunday worship. Others have darkened the doorway of a confessional after decades away from this sacrament. Still others have had a personal encounter with their Savior, Jesus, and the love of the Father in the power of the Holy Spirit. Using Sherry Weddell's language in her book *Forming Intentional*

Disciples—and that of the New Testament—these folks have experienced God and made the decision to "drop their nets." Scripture also says, "There will be more joy in heaven over one sinner who repents than over ninety-nine righteous persons who need no repentance" (Luke 15:7). Heaven is celebrating the return of these lost sheep! Yet too often we have spent more time counting the number of butts in the pews, bucks in the collection basket, and sacraments validly dispensed.

As a Senior Leadership Team, we developed a plan to publicly acknowledge those who have become disciples at Saint Benedict Parish. Pentecost seemed like a suitable time to do this, because it is the birthday of the Church, the day the Holy Spirit came in power.

At every Mass that Pentecost weekend, Fr. James invited forward all those who in the last twelve months could say, "Jesus changed my life!" Then he invited all those for whom this was true since the parish opened six years ago (in 2010). Counting all four Masses, a total of 107 and 352 people, respectively, stood up at the front of the church, witnessing to life transformation. It was a powerful moment for everyone present that weekend. Even better, there were about thirty teens who were being confirmed at the 9 a.m. Mass that day. When Fr. James made this invitation at that Mass, a few of the Confirmation candidates jumped out of their pews first! Do you judge them to be ready? I sure do. I love it when God's plan comes together; it is worth celebrating and keeping score.

What do I want you to know?

In chapter 17 I summarize the e-book *Keeping Score,* which speaks of our cultural tendency to measure all the wrong things. We need to clarify what defines missionary success. The things we measure and the things we celebrate are usually interconnected.

On the evening of Pentecost, we thought it would be appropriate to have an extended time of worship in the church. Many of the teenagers who were confirmed that morning returned to "praise their faces off." I was delighted to find myself worshipping God in the youth section that night; the faith and the level of engagement of these young people blew me away. Later I affirmed our youth minister, Ronnie Lunn, for his great work with the teens. He responded, "Praise God that we're not just growing in numbers but in disciples as well!"

What do I want you to do?

What took place at the Masses on that Pentecost Sunday has become an annual small "t" tradition at Saint Benedict. It is an opportunity for us to acknowledge and pray over those who are fresh on their journey. It also offers a beautiful witness to others who are sitting on the sidelines, resistant to change.

Pastors, with their lay leaders, should brainstorm a simple but effective way to recognize and affirm the people who are being evangelized through the parish. If you do call them forward at a Mass, be sure to have some volunteers ready to take photos, do a head count, and follow up afterwards.

CHAPTER 15

Naturally Supernatural

As a seminarian, I studied philosophy and theology at a Dominican college. Hence, you might expect me to be a Thomistic scholar. Sorry to disappoint you. I do remember a few random things about Aquinas, including the fact that he was super smart, liked angels, and had substantial girth. One of his famous axioms comes to mind: "Grace builds on nature." Fr. James emphasizes that we are not simply talking about grace *and* nature; God's supernatural grace thrives and grows on a solid natural foundation.

We were blessed to have Deacon Keith Strohm, an evangelist, parish consultant, and mission speaker, with us at Saint Benedict to lead our staff retreat and parish Lenten mission in 2016. He has served the Church in various ways and has been affiliated with the Catherine of Siena Institute. In addition to the evening mission talks, we had casual question-and-answer periods each morning after daily Mass. I was impressed by his grasp of theology and his ability to respond to difficult issues in a comprehensive way, with simple language and a dash of humor. Furthermore, Deacon Keith has been given a few of the more supernatural gifts that we read about in the New Testament (see 1 Corinthians 12), such as the gifts of prophecy, healing, and discernment of spirits. Needless to say, his ministry touched many, many people at our parish!

Our staff retreat was particularly grace-filled and right on target. I largely attribute that to the time Kate Robinson, our Director of Communications, invested in briefing Deacon Keith on our culture, our Game Plan, and our current situation. He challenged us, in a talk by the same name, to get back to "The Heart of the Matter." Namely, we all need to have intimacy with Jesus. As leaders we need to support and encourage our parish staff in this relationship with Jesus.

His sharing also gave me a heightened awareness that we are in a spiritual battle. Parishes that are attempting to become mission-oriented are high-value targets for the enemy. With this in mind, I am reminded of the urgent need for intercessors—people who are praying and fasting—as Jesus' kingdom is being established in greater ways on earth.

On a personal note, I enjoyed spending time with Deacon Keith and learned a lot from him. In fact, I felt so comfortable around him that I took the liberty of offering him some unsolicited feedback after the Saturday evening Mass. He spoke for less than ten minutes, so I encouraged him to "go for it" during the rest of the weekend Masses (our people are accustomed to fifteen-to-twenty-minute homilies on the weekend). He has an amazing ability to tell stories that are hilarious and communicate profound truths, and so I suggested that he use the extra time to share an amazing God story to connect with people and entice them to come out for the mission. He received the feedback with humility and made a few changes accordingly. As a result, the rest of his Sunday homilies were even richer, and there was a huge turnout for the mission.

To use a different example, I recall a powerful evening of prayer and ministry at our Companions of the Cross Community retreat in 2015. I thanked Fr. Scott McCaig afterwards for his leadership in this regard. He prayed ahead of time for

God's guidance and called forth a few brothers to help plan and facilitate the evening, which ended up being a profound encounter with the Holy Spirit. Nature and grace make a winning combination!

What do I want you to know?

We need to lead and prepare to the best of our ability in the natural realm. Then we need to surrender ourselves completely—giving God permission—and pray that the Holy Spirit will amplify our efforts in the supernatural.

Here is another Ron "Huntley-ism": "We can never not be coaching!" I will admit that it was bold of me to offer feedback to our guest preacher. To be fair, my desire was to explain our context and encourage his strengths so that the maximum amount of grace could be unleashed on our parish. In the end, Deacon Keith commented that the "secret sauce" at Saint Benedict is our implementation of the best practices from the leadership world combined with a sincere desire to help people experience the Holy Spirit.

What do I want you to do?

Many of us have a tendency toward one of two extremes.

Some chase after the signs and wonders without giving any regard to laying a firm natural foundation. If you lean toward this category, think about the next "Holy Spirit event" you might be planning. How can you best lead the team and those attending? Consider coaching the team ahead of time with clear instructions. During the event, offer guidance when necessary to allow the experience to be powerful without letting it become weird or chaotic.

Deacon Keith cautioned people at the other end of the spectrum, saying: "It is possible to minister almost exclusively out of the natural!" This latter disposition will yield a limited amount of fruit. If you find yourself in this category, pray for more boldness (see Acts 4, the Second Pentecost) and look for opportunities to step out in faith. Offering to pray with people as often as possible—after Mass, for example, or at dinner parties—is an easy way to start boldly stepping out. Whenever someone asks me to pray for a particular intention, I ask if we can pray together right then and there. Most people say yes. I always ask if I can lay a hand on their shoulder, and then I say a simple prayer from my heart, out loud. Every time I do this, my faith increases.

Creating a Game Plan

When it comes to parish life, change does not occur accidentally. As they say, hope is not a strategy. If we want to move our parishes from maintenance to mission, it will take concerted and intentional effort. The old adage, "If you want to go places you've never gone, you will have to do things you've never done," applies here.

But doing things we've never done does not mean trying new things randomly and creating busyness. Although that *can* yield some fruit, taking a more deliberate and focused approach to parish life will offer even greater results. At Saint Benedict, we call that deliberate, big-picture strategy our Game Plan. After a few years of hard work, gaining momentum in evangelization and discipleship, the team looked back and evaluated what was actually bearing fruit. These elements became the primary focus and were codified into an intentional, though not perfectly linear, path for making and growing disciples. Having a Game Plan makes it easier to evaluate events after they happen, and it also allows your leadership team to discern future opportunities that present themselves.

The following reflections are related to various components of our Game Plan, highlighting successes and pitfalls that we've experienced. I hope they will give you insight as you start to consider a big-picture strategy that could work in your situation.

CHAPTER 16

Defining the Win

Before I moved out to Nova Scotia to work at Saint Benedict, Fr. James asked me to take a thirty-minute online personality assessment tool that also takes social interactions into consideration (see the Birkman Method in the Resources section of this book). I did a follow-up phone interview with a Birkman coach, Brent Dolfo, who was already familiar with the parish. In fact, Brent helped Fr. James build the original Senior Leadership Team at Saint Benedict.

Let me take a moment to explain that a Senior Leadership Team is comparable to a team of executives or vice-presidents who use their collective wisdom and expertise to make the best decisions possible for an organization. It is crucial that this team, usually made up of four or five members, have a good balance of strengths and styles. When I started at Saint Benedict, I joined the Leadership Team that had been together for almost a year. It included Fr. James Mallon, pastor; Ron Huntley, Director of Pastoral Ministries (evangelization, discipleship, ministry); Rob McDowell, Director of Parish Life (administration, buildings, operations, systems); and Kate Robinson, Director of Communications (monthly publication in place of a weekly bulletin, social media, scheduling). I'll talk more about our Senior Leadership Team in future chapters because it has been so central to the ongoing success of the parish.

Going back to the Birkman interview, it offered a good refresher of my main strengths and weaknesses. I can be a bit of an "alpha male" (pun intended). I have been in charge at various times in the past, but I needed to be aware of my position as *associate* pastor. My primary reason for going to Saint Benedict was to learn so that I could facilitate parish renewal in a future assignment. The interview also reminded me that I have a preference for the pragmatic and hands-on rather than for thinking outside the box. Most important, the interview revealed that I am extremely success driven, so much so that I try to respond to the never-ending black hole of ministry needs. As an example, for every e-mail I conquer, ten more rise up in its place. The Birkman coach said that someone like me needs to ask this question: "What does a win look like in ministry?"

I can definitely point to people and ministries over the years that have been blessed by God through something I have said or done. But because I do not take the time to define what success looks like overall, it has never been clear if I am actually succeeding in ministry!

Prior to my time at Saint Benedict, one of the most formative periods of my priesthood was the three-year assignment as a university chaplain in Detroit that I discussed in other chapters. In that short time, through the grace of God and some trial and error, I witnessed explosive growth on campus.

Every semester at Wayne State University, we invited students to join a six-week small-group faith study developed by Catholic Christian Outreach, an evangelization-focused organization that works on college campuses. For a few semesters, our numbers had plateaued at around 80 to 100 people in faith study groups. With my student leaders, we decided to challenge ourselves to invite 130 people to join a group that January. It was bold and ambitious, but we managed to meet our target. We defined success very clearly, and we were able to achieve it. Looking back, we probably forgot to celebrate this huge victory, but at least it was a good start. Sadly, that is the only time that comes to mind from my past ministry when I set a clear objective and encouraged those around me to strive together toward the goal.

What do I want you to know?

First, make use of tools that can assess the personalities and strengths of individuals who are on, or who could end up on, your leadership team. This group of four or five key leaders cannot simply fall together haphazardly. They need to be intentionally built by finding the right mix and balance of gifted individuals.

Second, even if you are not as competitive as I am, I think that all of us will find ministry far more satisfying when we can see clearly if and when we are "winning."

What do I want you to do?

Take time with a pen and paper to clarify a few goals for your ministry this year. This exercise should be done individually and as a group. The leadership team as well as every ministry team in the parish should take time to step back and define the win.

The most intelligent people in the field suggest coming up with SMART goals: Specific, Measurable, Agreed upon, Realistic, and Time-bound.

When you do experience success, be sure to give thanks to God and celebrate with the key players who helped to make it happen.

CHAPTER 17

Keeping Score

Afriend told me this childhood story about Tim Tebow, a former NFL quarterback. One day his T-ball coach gave the team a pep talk about how it doesn't matter if you win or lose, it's only about having fun. Four-year-old Tim was confused. He yanked on the man's shirt and said, "No, coach, you're wrong. It's only about winning. That's when you have fun." The coach called Tim's dad over to scold his son for being overly competitive. His dad leaned down and whispered, "Timmy, he just doesn't understand." It seems like that fatherly encouragement had a lasting impact.

Ron Huntley, also the father of a successful athlete—his son has played in the Quebec Major Junior Hockey League—recommended that I read the short e-book *Keeping Score: How to Know If Your Church Is Winning* by Dave Ferguson. Given my own competitive nature and desire to see the Church win, this resource has been invaluable. The following is a summary of a few main concepts.

First, the author makes it clear that winning worldly achievements is different from winning for the kingdom of God. What matters most to God is faithfulness. As Matthew 25:21 says, "Well done, good and faithful servant." But to what are we called to be faithful? I think the Great Commission is summarized most simply in these two words: make disciples. This entails transforming people, marriages, and families. Eternity is in the balance, and so as Church leaders we can't just play for fun. The truth is that we all care more about the results when we are keeping score.

Yet the majority of churches do not measure what matters most. Traditionally we count the number of nickels and noses (collection and attendance), which are helpful statistics to be aware of but do not directly speak to discipleship. Success in a parish context can be boiled down to this statement: "If you are making disciples, your church will win. If you do not make disciples, your church will lose."

In recent years, the word *disciple* has come back into fashion in the Catholic world. Most Catholics have a vague sense that this term refers to a follower of Christ. In order to keep track of the disciples in our parishes, it is up to the pastor and his lay leaders to clearly define what they understand by this term. Community Christian Church in Chicago describes the process of disciple making as "apprenticing people in the ways of Jesus." They like that term "disciple making" because "it implies a relational way of learning that includes both knowing and doing."

You can't just become a disciple by passing a test in a classroom. Discipleship is a lifestyle, and therefore it possesses characteristics—patterns of life—that can be clearly identified and observed. Some of these characteristics include attending church weekly, praying daily, reading Sacred Scripture, entering into worship regularly, participating in a small group, attending adult faith formation courses, serving at the parish and in the broader community, being financially generous, placing Jesus at the center of one's life, sharing faith with others, and so forth.

What do I want you to know?

What we measure reveals our priorities and our motives. If the only thing we measure without fail (and publish weekly in the bulletin) is the collection, what does that say about what we value as a church? We need to begin to measure what matters most to Jesus: disciples.

What do I want you to do?

A pastor and his leadership team should take an honest look at the things the parish is currently measuring. Are these connected directly or indirectly to the mission of Jesus? Brainstorm a list of some things you should be measuring. Most people are content with an ambiguous feeling of improvement, but be specific. If you are going to measure something, you should be able to put a number to it.

Ron, Kate, and I did this exercise and came up with the following list: number of people in Alpha (percent unchurched, percent under 35); number of people in Connect Groups, Discipleship Groups, and serving in ministry; weekly Mass attendance; total giving (percent through automatic withdrawal); percent of the budget allocated to the mission as opposed to maintenance. At the top of the list was the number of people in the last twelve months who can say, "Jesus has made a difference in my life."

You might want to begin by defining discipleship at your parish. After painting the picture of what a disciple looks like, choose between three and seven characteristics that are most important for your community. Then create a spreadsheet so that your team can keep track of the number of people who are growing in discipleship and, specifically, which characteristics they are currently living. For example, a person might be going to Mass weekly but might not be reading the Bible daily. If you have an awareness of which discipleship characteristics are most deficient, you can start to make a plan to address whatever is missing.

I recommend reading *Keeping Score* (see the Resources section).

The Bigger They Are . . .

Joe Walcott, the welterweight boxing world champion from 1901 to 1904, coined the phrase "The bigger they are, the harder they fall." However, when it comes to Catholic parishes, it seems like the following would be more accurate: "The bigger they are, the more we do things exactly the same."

Toward the end of *Divine Renovation*, Fr. James refers to an article by Timothy Keller titled "Leadership and Church Size Dynamics: How Strategy Changes with Growth." This fifteen-page article, which can be found online, is full of insights about how size really does matter when it comes to leading parishes. The following is a brief overview of a few key concepts.

Parishes are classified according to their average Sunday attendance: house church (up to 40), small church (40–200), medium-sized church (200–450), large church (400–800), and very large church (800+). In my estimation, a typical urban or suburban Catholic parish would be categorized as a large, if not a very large, church. And I suspect that it would likely be limited by small church structures and attitudes. For example, Keller states that "in small churches policy is decided by many and ministry is done by a few, while in the large church, ministry is done by many and policy is decided by a few." Conversely, I know of several very large Catholic parishes where a small number of people are doing all the ministry; meanwhile, everyone wants to have a say in the decision-making process.

There are advantages and disadvantages to any church size. Keller says, "The reason for being in a smaller church is relationships. The reason for putting up with all the changes and difficulties of a larger church is to get mission done." As a parish grows in size, it needs to consider some of the following: being more systematic about welcoming newcomers, being more intentional and clear around communication, providing higher-quality production (including music and preaching), offering small groups for fellowship and growth, and adding staff and shifting their responsibilities.

With regard to music in a small church, people are willing to put up with a few songs sung off-key if they know the musician personally. When it comes to preaching, there is a similar dynamic in place: "While in a larger church people will let you pastor them if you are a good preacher, in a smaller church the reverse is true: people will listen to your sermons if you are a good pastor." On another note, when people from a small church (or a parish with a "small-church attitude") join a church with over 1,000 parishioners, they might be surprised that they are unable to speak directly to the pastor on the phone when they have a need. They will have to grow in patience and adjust to a larger church context.

When I was on campus in Detroit, we started out as the equivalent of a house church and grew to the small church category. Early on I felt the need for at least one lay staff person to help with pastoring but was only offered administrative help. We were being pigeonholed into a house-church-sized culture, and it impeded our growth. If you have the freedom, be sure your next hire will grow the church and increase the giving (to allow for future staff hires).

What do I want you to know?

We tend to place a moral status on our preferred church size. Many people feel at home in a small church community, while others like the feeling of being part of something huge that is having an impact on the world.

As a church grows, the staff will have to become more and more specialized in their particular domains, and processes will have to be developed accordingly. For example, the pastor will have to delegate teams to work with people who are knocking on the church doors seeking sacraments. Perhaps of greatest significance, the pastor will have to focus primarily on growing in the areas of preaching, communicating the vision so that others buy into it, and strategizing. He will need a strong staff around him to take care of a lot of the other details and hands-on ministry.

What do I want you to do?

Instead of just reading Timothy Keller's article, a pastor and his lay leaders should take the time to carefully study the points that he presents.

As you read, assess your parish and its culture in terms of church size and growth. Believe that God wants your church to grow! It is important to understand the dynamics of the next size category so you can start to prepare your people for change.

See *Divine Renovation* (pp. 260–263) for more of Fr. James' comments on this article.

CHAPTER 19

Here and There (Part 1 of 2)

Minutes before the 6 p.m. Mass one Sunday, I noticed a few familiar faces from Ottawa in the Saint Benedict foyer. Three young adults had made the grueling fifteen-hour drive to visit one of their siblings who had recently moved to Halifax. They decided to check out the famous Divine Renovation church while they were in town. Given that it was the evening Mass on Canadian Thanksgiving (and most parishioners were probably at home in a turkey-induced coma), I found myself apologizing for the thin crowd and what was likely to be a less-than-epic Mass experience. That evening Mass has a lower attendance on any given Sunday anyway and tends to draw people who are just passing through. It can feel somewhat average.

I share this not to be critical and negative but to recognize that Saint Benedict is very much a work in progress. This is a truly exciting place to be ministering, yet there are still many areas in need of improvement. We regularly have tough conversations as a Senior Leadership Team about where we are as a community so that we remain realistic about the "here" because we are not "there" yet.

Understanding and measuring where things stand in a parish is a good place to start. In *Divine Renovation*, Fr. James refers to the ME[25] survey, which was created by Gallup. You can read more about this in Albert Winseman's book *Growing an Engaged Church: How to Stop "Doing Church" and Start Being the Church Again.* The survey tries to measure the level of member engagement (emotional connection to the parish) by identifying three groups: the engaged (those paddling the canoe forward), the actively disengaged (those paddling backwards against the vision and strategy), and the unengaged (those who are generally content to just go along for the ride).

The ME[25] does come with a modest price tag, so a parish needs to see it as a long-term investment in their overall spiritual health. Saint Benedict Parish has used it five times so far, around once every eighteen months. One great advantage of a survey is that it will create hard data around the anonymous responses of the people sitting in your pews. When referencing it later, the pastor will not merely have to go with his gut feeling but be able to point to real numbers.

Another simple way to begin to identify the "here" could be through doing a SWOT exercise with a group of staff and lay leaders who have the pulse of the parish—the parish council, perhaps. Begin by making four quadrants on a board or a flip chart to represent Strengths, Weaknesses, Opportunities, and Threats. Come up with a list of items that fall into each category. The Strengths and Weaknesses should focus on the lived experience at the parish right now, whereas the Opportunities and Threats are connected to future realities.

One way to break it down further might be to do five separate SWOT exercises, one for each of the five systems that Rick Warren speaks about in his book *The Purpose Driven Church*: Worship, Evangelization, Discipleship, Fellowship, and Ministry. How are things going in each of these vital areas of parish life? Doing a visual exercise with a group of people you trust can help to clarify the "here" in a way that will be very useful as you start to move your community forward toward the destination: "There."

What do I want you to know?

Rob McDowell, the Director of Parish Life at Saint Benedict, often reminds us that one of the first responsibilities of a leader is to define reality. He is referencing *Leadership Is an Art*, by Max Depree. The quote continues: "The last is to say thank you. In between the two, the leader must become a servant." It is premature to begin to move the parish forward in a particular direction if you have not taken the time to try to understand the "here."

What do I want you to do?

All of us have a vague sense of where there are holes in ministries and what is falling apart or dysfunctional. Still, it is important to invest some time (and if you go with the ME[25], some resources) in measuring the status of the parish as it stands today. One of the great benefits, down the road, is that you will be able to celebrate the wins because you will be able to clearly see how far the parish has grown in the areas where it was once weak.

Book an hour or two with your staff and lay leaders and work through a SWOT exercise. You may wish to use Rick Warren's five systems or the ten values that Fr. James has listed in *Divine Renovation* as a framework for your discussions:

1. Giving Priority to the Weekend
2. Hospitality
3. Uplifting Music
4. Great Homilies

5. Meaningful Community

6. Clear Expectations

7. Strength-Based Ministry

8. Formation of Small Communities

9. Experience of the Holy Spirit

10. Become an Inviting Church

See the *Divine Renovation Guidebook* for a Ten Values Analysis exercise (pp. 74–78).

See the *Divine Renovation Guidebook* for a SWOT Analysis Exercise for the Five Systems (pp. 89–104).

CHAPTER 20

Going at Full Gallup

Fr. James and I were invited to a gathering of church leaders in the Halifax area. A great deal of planning and promotion was under way in preparation for an international Alpha campaign featuring Bear Grylls. He is a famous adventure seeker who, in one episode of his show *Man vs. Wild*, took Will Ferrell up to the Swedish Artic for a forty-eight-hour survival challenge. It's cool enough that this guy can rappel out of helicopters at subzero temperatures, but even more impressive is the fact that he's taken the risk to go public about his Christian faith.

The main speaker at this Alpha promotion event began by presenting a lot of statistics; he was defining reality! Christian churches across the board are in decline, which is no surprise to anyone. In 1945, 64 percent of Canadians were at church every week. In 2013, that number was 11 percent. Yet even those who have little or no involvement in their churches still have some denominational loyalty. The speaker stated that 37 percent of Canadians are Catholic. He went on to say that 87 percent of Roman Catholics (outside of Quebec) are not open to switching traditions. For mainline Protestants, that number is 75 percent, and for Conservative Evangelicals it is 81 percent. In other words, if people were to go back to church, they would likely go back to "their" church. By looking at the numbers, our non-Catholic presenter was convinced that the best hope for Canada is for us to work together across denominations.

An aside: though most of us say the phone line is *busy*, I remember as a child hearing my dad say that the line is *engaged* (the British Bear Grylls probably says the same thing). It means that two parties are connected. This relates to something I recently read in Albert Winseman's book *Growing an Engaged Church* (Gallup Press). Winseman writes convincingly of the need for engagement in our communities. In fact, he points out, "Neurological research confirms that our emotional connections are far stronger than our rational connections" (p. 30). More than just knowing that an organization or church is great, we have to *feel* it! Furthermore, much of the research recognizes that a turning point or a kind of born-again experience plays a significant part in increasing a person's overall emotional engagement.

Here are a few other insights I have gleaned from the book. (By the way, I found the author to be sensitive to and considerate of Catholics.) According to the research, the four most relevant indicators of a church's spiritual health are life satisfaction, inviting, serving, and giving. This spiritual health, in turn, comes from two main causes: *spiritual commitment* (a personal reality) and *congregational engagement.* Spiritual commitment deals with things like a person's inner peace, prayer life, ability to forgive others, and so forth. Sadly, concerning congregational engagement, the author said, "It seems that deep, meaningful relationships are not being formed in most congregations" (p. 104).

People get engaged when expectations are clear, their spiritual needs are met, they are able to do what they do best, they feel cared for by the spiritual leaders, and so on. Congregational engagement can be summarized by these four questions: What do I get? What do I give? Do I belong? How can we grow?

Here is the bottom line: "If you can't measure it, you can't manage it" (p. 33).

What do I want you to know?

Ron Huntley often reminds me that Jesus cared about numbers, and so should we (take, for example, the ninety-nine sheep and the one that was lost). Ignoring current Church trends in the West is as misguided as one finding out that one is extremely prone to a heart attack but continuing on with business as usual, optimistic that things will get better on their own. If you still feel uncomfortable leaning into numbers in the parish context, Winseman reminds us that they "aren't just statistics to me. They represent personal stories" (p. 2).

The Gallup research suggests that, contrary to what you might intuitively think, overall spiritual health begins with congregational engagement; one of the fruits of this belonging is spiritual commitment (believing). In the past, we have tended to try to help people grow in spiritual commitment (proper belief), hoping that that, in itself, will make our church communities healthy. Finally, the three biggest causes of a downward drift in engagement are a change in the senior pastor, a change in worship times, and a change in worship styles.

What do I want you to do?

As a quick review, the ME[25] member engagement survey classifies people into three categories: engaged, not engaged (generally content, but along for the ride), and actively disengaged. The last group is also known as C.A.V.E. Dwellers (Consistently

Against Virtually Everything). It's in your best interests not to spend too much time on them. Focus your energy on helping the not-engaged move into engagement. The best chance for a C.A.V.E. Dweller is if a formerly not-engaged person witnesses to them, pulling them up into the light.

Albert Winseman offers these three practical recommendations for increasing congregational engagement (p. 125):

- Clarify the expectations of membership.
- Help your members discover what they do best.
- Create small groups.

CHAPTER 21

Here and There (Part 2 of 2)

consider myself a realist, a pragmatist, and a hard worker. Maybe it is because I am hardwired that way, but I have always struggled with the notion of capturing and communicating a vision—that is, "casting vision." Secretly I envy those who are natural visionaries, because every priest in a leadership position is responsible for casting vision. Bill Hybels, a gifted visionary and the lead pastor at Willow Creek Community Church, defines it this way: "Vision is a picture of the future that produces passion." I was talking with a Saint Benedict staff member recently about how to build ministry teams. She reemphasized that rather than merely asking people to help fill a need, we invite them to join in the dream. As Hybels would say, help them to understand the "White-Hot Why."

So how do you start to fix your eyes on the horizon? Fr. James speaks of finding the itch and then scratching it until it bothers you so much, you have to look beyond for a solution. I was whining to Ron Huntley the other day about how I really struggle with this vision piece. He got in my grill and started asking really tough questions about what bothers me. Why? Who cares? In the moment, I spoke to the frustration of looking out on Sunday—even at a wonderful church like Saint Benedict—and seeing so many "parochial zombies." I was reminded of how much fun it is when people experience new life in Christ. Imagine if more and more people in the pews were being awakened with God's abundant life (see John 10:10). What kind of missionary impact could that have on the parish, and beyond the church walls, if people began to encounter and share the love of Jesus? That is just the beginning of a developing picture of the future.

Leadership is directional. Leaders move people! Bill Hybels captures this concept beautifully in his talk "From Here to There." In part 1, I wrote about defining the "here" first. Rather than pointing to the "there" right away, Hybels suggests that we start by focusing on how bad it is *here*. In the Catholic context, the Church is hemorrhaging parishioners, folks come for sacraments and are "one-and-done," parishes are notoriously cold and inhospitable, many people are just going through the religious motions, and so on. Fr. Bob Bedard, the founder of the Companions of the Cross, would often touch this very sensitive nerve: so many of our children and grandchildren have left the faith—are you okay with that? If you paint the picture for people so they can see how bad things are, they might be convinced and cry out, "We can't stay here!" It is at that point that you can present a vision of a better future that people will be willing to embrace.

If you spend a lot of time in the trenches, you can easily forget why you have been working so hard. By reconnecting with the vision of the future, you can recalibrate and continue to drive forward.

What do I want you to know?

As with most leadership principles, vision is not necessarily a gift we are born with but an area that can be developed. Bill Hybels started the Global Leadership Summit as an annual event to gather leaders and to refill their vision tanks. We all have a tendency to leak. This year everyone was challenged to become 5 percent better as a leader in the coming year.

I dream of a Church full of bishops, priests, and lay people who display excellence in leadership and who are raising up a generation of missionary disciples.

What do I want you to do?

Spend some time wrestling with the vision for your parish. If you are intimidated by the responsibility of visioning, the good news is that God grants us more than we could ask or imagine (see Ephesians 3:20). Spend extended times in prayer begging him for a future picture of your parish that will fill you and your people with passion.

Get together with other priests and with lay leaders and ask one another to articulate what bothers them. Why is that particular thing so important? Is it the most important itch?

My first attempt at creating a vision statement was during my time as chaplain at Wayne State University. We started by brainstorming picture words with a group of student leaders and crafted this in 2013–2014:

> We see our **upper room** as a place **burning** with Catholic **renewal,** where **young adults** are **drawn in** by the **faithful community** and the **dynamic prayer** and **worship,** where they are consistently being led to **conversion** to the **person of Jesus** and being formed as His **followers,** and where they are **freely** and **enthusiastically** responding to the call to be **disciple makers.**

CHAPTER 22

Peeking at the Playbook

Thinking about Super Bowl Sunday reminds me of a sports analogy. Every successful football coaching staff has some kind of a playbook with all their best strategies drawn out with Xs and Os and arrows. When I was a kid, I would attend our weekly altar boys' group on Saturday mornings. After Mass, a spiritual reflection, and snacks, the lot of us went outside to play tackle football. Just like the pros, we would have a huddle, and the quarterback would draw out the play on the palm of his hand. Usually speed and brawn won the day, but every once in a while, a crazy double-fake hand-off created a distraction, while another guy went long to catch an incredible Hail Mary pass. Catholic boys will be Catholic boys.

Looking back on my limited priestly experience, I recall my first assignment in a parish when everything was exciting and new. When it came to making disciples, it was almost by accident that I was able to see a little fruit. Upon arriving at the campus in Detroit, with almost nothing happening I had the freedom to focus on the following three areas: the sacraments, Catholic Christian Outreach faith studies, and the Upper Room—a weekly event with a talk, fellowship, Eucharistic adoration, and contemporary worship. These three priorities helped students to encounter Jesus in the power of the Holy Spirit and to receive the healing and mercy of God the Father. After leaving Detroit, I had a few other brief experiences of parishes that were very much in maintenance mode. For example, one church was sinking most of its time and resources into resurrecting its rotten church steeple (how symbolic).

At Saint Benedict, it is refreshing to be part of a team that is trying to be intentional about the mission of Jesus. To bring this about, the team developed a big-picture strategy. Rather than beginning with a plan, the staff has been evaluating what has been bearing fruit over the last few years. This has been systematized into a transferable process. We call it the Game Plan.

To be clear, this is not meant to be a linear process but a general path that has multiple entry points. If you are familiar with Alpha, you will notice that all the icons are based on the red Alpha question mark. This is because Alpha, a welcoming evangelization process geared toward those with little church background or experience, is so central to our missionary endeavors. Getting people to Alpha presupposes that we are fostering a culture of invitation where it becomes normal for everyone in our parish to invite non-Catholics, non-Christians, and the lukewarm to experience something new.

After attending Alpha, the most joyful and engaged people there are invited back to serve on the next Alpha team, offering hospitality and facilitating faith-based discussions for the next round of guests. This helps individuals develop a heart for others, grow deeper in faith and confidence, and invest more deeply in our parish.

Eventually we encourage Alpha grads to join a midsized Connect Group of twenty to thirty people where they can continue to grow in the context of a supportive community. Connect Group leaders challenge their members to serve in a parish ministry and to participate in a short-term Discipleship Group of about four to ten people once a year. Over the

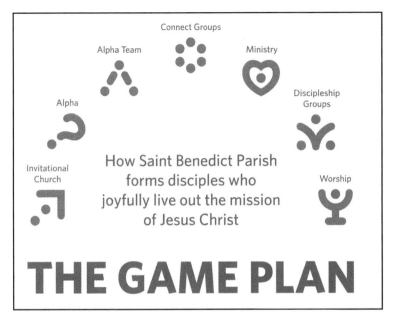

Connect Groups

Alpha Team

Ministry

Alpha

Discipleship Groups

Invitational Church

Worship

How Saint Benedict Parish forms disciples who joyfully live out the mission of Jesus Christ

THE GAME PLAN

course of about four to ten weeks, Discipleship Groups gather for a Bible study or another form of content-driven formation (the image represents both a book and a growing plant). Ultimately, all are called to worship and to the sacraments (the image represents both a person with arms raised praising God and a host and chalice).

Sadly, the game plan for many parishes is hoping that people will attend Mass. A small percentage of these might serve in a ministry and may or may not join the occasional study group. The question arises: Are we implementing a strategy and scoring touchdowns, or are we throwing Hail Marys and hoping for the best? The most fruitful parishes create pastoral strategies that offer pathways to conversion and growth, so that men and women can encounter Christ and become missionary disciples. This becomes the focus of the life and activity of the community.

What do I want you to know?

I used to believe that only non-parish ministries, like university chaplaincies, had the freedom to focus the lion's share of their energy on evangelization. Parishes are bogged down by so many other "trappings." It seemed like parishes could do a little evangelizing on the side, as long as they were taking care of all that other important stuff.

Now I know that it is possible for a parish to create and follow a big-picture strategy designed to make disciples—under the power of the Holy Spirit.

What do I want you to do?

Take a close look at the different elements of our Game Plan and how they all fit together. The previous reflections in this section of the book are meant to help you prepare for this important work. We in no way believe that every church needs to follow our playbook page by page. On the other hand, there is no need to reinvent the wheel, so feel free to use this as a starting point.

Priests should meet with their key lay leaders to discuss a big-picture strategy for the parish. Use a whiteboard or a flip chart to draw a few versions of a mission-focused game plan that could work in your context.

See the Resources section for a homily I gave as we unveiled our Saint Benedict Game Plan.

CHAPTER 23

An Evangelization Invitation

Agood friend of mine, Michael Dopp, once gave a talk on evangelization at the parish where I was first assigned. He told a story about a time he went for a haircut and the woman asked what he was using on his hair. As I recall, it was some dollar-store variety of hair gel, probably not different from the kind I used to use—when I had hair. Given his hair type, she was shocked and started to share about the benefits of a product called "hair mud." She spoke enthusiastically about how it would change his life. She said, "I want to make it my mission in life to make sure guys use the right hair products."

What is your mission in life? Do you talk about it joyfully?

Fr. Bob Bedard was filled with radical zeal when it came to the mission of sharing the Gospel. Concerning evangelization, Fr. Bob came up with a three-step dynamic (see the Resources section). To begin, a Christian shares the Good News with another person in a way that he or she can respond. The second step, we hope, involves the person's wholehearted positive response. Finally, the Holy Spirit goes to work within the heart of the individual. By analogy, Gabriel proclaimed good news to Mary at the Annunciation and waited for a response. Mary offered her total *fiat* ("Let it be done"). As soon as she gave God permission, the Holy Spirit overshadowed her and Jesus was made present within her.

We are responsible for step one. The key is to share Good News *and* provide a concrete way for the other person to respond. Sadly, I can recall an occasion right before I joined the seminary when I shared my entire story of conversion with a high school friend. He, a fallen-away Catholic, hung on every word and was deeply moved by the end of it. He thanked me. I thanked him for listening. Then we went our separate ways. I completely missed the opportunity to give him a way to respond to my story of Good News. Similarly, homilies often move hearts but fail to evoke a response.

We'll take a closer look at Alpha in the next two chapters, but if you've been following along, by now you know that at Saint Benedict we offer Alpha as a gentle but concrete way for a person to respond. Every few months, we remind our people from the pulpit to invite friends and family to try Alpha. We reinforce this message with lay witnesses at Mass. Fr. James says that inviting someone to check out a dinner party, with a relevant message and a discussion, is the easiest ask he has ever had to make (we also make a point of serving delicious food at Alpha!).

I have invited several people to consider Alpha, and most have declined. Recently one fellow exclaimed, "I will NEVER EVER take Alpha!" As I cautiously backed away, I realized that it was good for me to experience a little rejection. This is what potentially awaits courageous parishioners who make the effort to invite. Rob McDowell, the Director of Parish Life at Saint Benedict, once said that there is a difference between understanding the Good News with our intellect and responding to that same Good News with our will. The latter is the ultimate goal.

What do I want you to know?

This may be obvious, but there is only one way for our parishes to grow, and that is when more people start coming to church. Statistically, the best way to attract people to your church—and to Jesus—is not through witty church signs (though I do enjoy them). The best tactic is the personal invitation. In the past, I have put pressure on myself to know how to articulate a clear and simple Gospel message at the drop of a hat. Of course, we should learn and practice sharing the Good News. But it is much easier to invite someone into a safe and fun environment where they will hear this message proclaimed little by little.

One of the hardest parts of evangelization is being willing to put out a personal invitation. As with a wedding invitation, we can and should seek a response.

What do I want you to do?

Do you have something going on in your parish to which friends and family members can be invited? Where can an unevangelized person go to have an encounter with God? You might consider making Alpha (or an equivalent approach) periodically available at your parish. This will provide a means through which people can respond. As Ron likes to say, "People who have an experience on Alpha start inviting their friends. Before they even know what they are doing, their friends are being evangelized!"

I would add that leaders have to lead by example. As priests and lay leaders, you need to model the invitation by stepping out of your comfort zones to invite the unchurched. Whenever I challenge parishioners to invite others, I try to share personal stories of invitations I have made. Some are successful, but as I said, many seem to flop. I make it clear that even though I am a priest, I am not particularly good at inviting or evangelizing. Still, I do it out of obedience to Jesus and because I love to see lives being changed.

See the Resources section for a talk and another homily I gave on this topic in the spring of 2016.

CHAPTER 24

Voyage to Alpha Centauri (Part 1 of 2)

Those who have heard of the self-taught Catholic painter and author Michael D. O'Brien might recognize the title of this reflection. I feel that I grow spiritually every time I read one of O'Brien's deep, thought-provoking novels.

Speaking of depth, Bishop Michael Byrnes, a former auxiliary bishop of the Archdiocese of Detroit, was once preaching in reference to our call to "put out into the deep" (Luke 5:4). He remarked that the Catholic Mass is *deep*—and very often this is exactly where we bring the unchurched or unevangelized. Rather than throw these people into the deep end, he suggested that we try to gently lead them to shallow-water entry points.

The Alpha evangelization process is one of these low-key, nonthreatening environments that is ideal for those who have been away from the practice of the faith or those who have never had any faith at all. A typical Alpha night has three components: a meal, a relevant talk, and a small-group discussion. My first exposure to Alpha was during my first year of seminary, when we watched the videos on VHS during our novitiate. I can still remember the dated hairdos and the touch of subtle English humor. (A brand-new version was released in 2016. Called the Alpha Film Series, it was filmed on-site all over the world with state of the art cinematography.)

In my early months in Halifax, I was immersed in the Alpha culture. Fr. James and Ron have been putting on Alphas—and learning from their mistakes—for the last fifteen years or so. The course runs a few times a year. From my vantage point, it serves as a tool for evangelization (making disciples) and allows for a discipleship process—ongoing growth, especially for those who return as part of the team. Through Alpha, new people can be coached step-by-step into positions of greater ministry responsibility. Our goal is to create several of these leadership pipelines at the parish. Those who have had a powerful experience on Alpha end up being the leaven at our *deep* liturgical Sunday gatherings—bringing a joyful tone, particularly when it comes to hospitality.

Here are two realizations I have come to concerning Alpha. First, the parishioners in the pews are not the primary target audience. Alpha is designed to be a safe place for an unchurched person to have a positive first impression of the faith and to come into an encounter with Jesus. Be sure to target the lost! If parishioners would like to participate, they will also be blessed, but they should be encouraged to invite their friends and family members to join them. It is a huge mistake to use Alpha solely as a program for deepening the faith of committed Catholics.

Second, Alpha is not the final destination, nor should it be expected to offer a comprehensive course on every tenet of Catholicism. As the name suggests, it is only the beginning. Getting people into midsized Connect Groups of about twenty to thirty people is essential in helping new disciples continue to grow in their relationship with God as they forge lasting relationships with other faithful disciples.

What do I want you to know?

We need to ensure that our parishes have a shallow end. It is so important to have an effective disciple-making system in place, with a particular outward focus toward the lost.

Fr. Bob Bedard advised the Companions of the Cross to look to see what the Holy Spirit is blessing and then go and stand next to it. In previous decades, in a more Christian society, other evangelization tools have been very effective. I know that some do not appreciate the comparison, but I can see the similarity between a Life in the Spirit Seminar and an Alpha, between a prayer meeting and a Connect Group. One of the main differences is that Alpha and Connect Groups both involve food; I am all for that. Could this be where the Holy Spirit is blowing today?

What do I want you to do?

I encourage you to familiarize yourself with Alpha. (See the Resources section, which includes a few Divine Renovation podcasts featuring Fr. James and Ron.) You can also find all of the Alpha videos online. Some of you might be interested in the Alpha Youth Film Series for teens, which is slightly shorter and geared toward a younger audience (nevertheless, Nicky Gumbel, the Anglican priest who developed Alpha, is timeless). Again, the Alpha videos are available in high definition for free on YouTube!

Spend some time learning before launching your Alpha. Keep in mind that the main reason people never return to Alpha is because of a bad small-group experience. I would suggest investing time with the online training videos and using them to help coach the table hosts and helpers. Running an Alpha *well* can make all the difference.

CHAPTER 25

Voyage to Alpha Centauri (Part 2 of 2)

In September 2015, I got to visit Holy Trinity Brompton (HTB), the Anglican church in London where Alpha was first developed. There were six Catholics in the group of about fifty church leaders, all attending a conference. Most were pastors and leaders from Christian megachurches, with many, but not all, located on the West Coast of the United States. There were representatives from two other Catholic churches besides Saint Benedict: Our Lady of Good Counsel, Fr. John Riccardo's parish near Detroit, Michigan, and Saint Ann, near Dallas, Texas. (Saint Ann has since joined the Divine Renovation Network. Over the years I have preached at Our Lady of Good Counsel, and I have visited Saint Ann's Parish. It's a small Catholic world!)

Jen Ferrier, our former staff member who coordinated Alpha, and I connected with the folks from these parishes, sharing ideas and being mutually edified. It was good to network with leaders from other Catholic churches who were asking the right questions about the mission of the Church—how to make disciples—and actively searching for answers. I had a blast exploring London, experiencing a few English pubs, and being on the receiving end of "radical hospitality," which is part of the culture modeled by the staff at HTB. During the conference, we were immersed in the history of HTB. I was surprised to learn that John Wimber, an American involved with founding the Vineyard Movement, had been influential at the church.

We had the opportunity to meet several of the original key players at HTB: Nicky and Pippa Gumbel, Nicky and Sila Lee (creators of the Marriage Course), and Anglican Bishop Sandy Miller. After Bishop Miller's sharing, he asked to pray over the group. In a very unassuming, simple style, he called upon the Holy Spirit. Later, he made his way through the crowd and eventually reached me. Before I could say a word, he acknowledged that HTB has been blessed by many Catholics over the years, including Fr. Raniero Cantalamessa, preacher to the papal household. I asked him to pray for me as a representative of my entire religious community. His loving, grandfatherly demeanor was so familiar. I feel that the role Bishop Sandy played for the Anglican Church in England, at the outset of the renewal, was similar to the role that Fr. Bob Bedard played for the Catholic Church in Canada during that same period.

What was my greatest highlight? Midway through the first day, the facilitator invited the six Catholics to the front and asked the other church leaders to pray over us. They took turns speaking, but the very first senior pastor said something like, "On behalf of all of us children of the Reformation, who act as though the Church was founded only five hundred years ago, I want to repent." Hot tears started rolling down my cheeks—which is totally out of character for me. I was invited to witness to this experience the following morning in front of about 250 people at the HTB/Alpha staff meeting. I also took the opportunity to repent, on behalf of myself and all Catholics, for being prideful and for passing judgment on our Christian brothers and sisters. After visiting HTB, it became so evident to me that our fellow Christians want to see the Catholic Church come alive.

What do I want you to know?

God's grace is upon HTB. In addition to the above experiences, I saw 850 people (200 of whom were on the team) in their twenties and thirties participating in an Alpha, on a Wednesday night, in the middle of downtown secularized London.

I was chatting with fellow Canadian Jason Ballard, of Alpha Youth Film Series fame, over fish and chips one evening. I think he is in his late twenties, though he still looks like a teenager but speaks with the authority of someone twice his age. He said that 100 years from now, when they write the history books, Alpha will be known not so much as an evangelization tool but as a movement of Christian unity. I felt incredibly honored in my priesthood during my visit to Holy Trinity Brompton. It is hard for me to admit, but a few of the veteran priests in my religious community who are passionate about ecumenism might actually be on to something.

What do I want you to do?

Repent of your own attitudes and judgments toward Christians of other traditions, and pray for God's blessing upon them. Keep an eye out for a nearby Christian church that has been successful at moving from maintenance to mission. Consider going out for coffee with a pastor or leader from such a church to learn what you can from their model and their growth.

Pray about making a "pilgrimage" to London to visit HTB for one of their conferences. There is nothing quite like being inspired firsthand. Sometimes we need to see something with our own eyes in order to believe, "This is actually possible!"

CHAPTER 26

Connecting the Dots

In the spring of 2016, we had a visit from a brother Companion priest, Fr. Yves Marchildon, a man with a huge pastor's heart. It was an exploratory mission to see what is feeding the sheep at Saint Benedict Parish.

Fr. Yves took in plenty of different meetings and Masses at the parish, but his primary goal was to learn about Connect Groups, which are represented on our Saint Benedict Game Plan as a circle of dots. These midsized groups meet in parishioners' homes every two weeks. They offer a safe place for people to be supported by a loving community as they grow in faith and prayer. Individuals can also develop various spiritual gifts in this context. For some, it is the first time they pray non-scripted prayers or speak in front of a crowd. Connect Groups are a natural continuation of the Alpha experience and include a meal, an icebreaker, a witness or talk from a group member, small-group discussions, and a time of worship and intercession. Going to a Connect Group is like going to a Christian dinner party! Based on the amount of laughter I have witnessed at Connect Groups, they are meant to be a lot of fun.

A different but wonderful mix of church folk invited me over for dinner recently. Knowing that they are all into music, I decided to take my giant Companions of the Cross guitar-chord binder. As the night progressed, we ate, we talked, we drank, and then we ate, we talked, and we drank some more. The drinking was in moderation, though I cannot say the same for the eating and the chatter. Much of the conversation was interesting and inspiring, but as the night went on, I found it had grown mundane. I excused myself before I turned into a pumpkin, and took my unused music binder home with me. I'm pretty sure that if I had asked the people at that dinner party if they would have felt more fulfilled had we shifted gears and spent some of the evening in prayer and worship, they would have said yes unanimously. What our gathering lacked was a little bit of shepherding and some basic structure.

After visiting a few different Connect Groups, Fr. Yves and I were amazed that the participants look forward to this event as a biweekly highlight and a spiritual lifeline. At Saint Benedict, there are currently about 325 parishioners spread across twelve groups, generally arranged according to their stage in life. The parents of young children look forward to connecting with other parents, while the kids love to hang out with their friends from the parish. It is a win-win situation for everyone, but the biggest winners are the priests! Without any direct clergy involvement, each Connect Group flock is being tended and fed by four trusted lay leaders. These leaders, in essence, act as small "p" pastors.

What do I want you to know?

I recently visited a Connect Group and noticed a woman I had seen at Alpha a few months earlier. I was pleasantly surprised to see this timid person trying out a Connect Group for the first time. She decided to give it a shot after hearing a homily I gave during Lent. I explained our seven-icon Game Plan and remarked that the keystone (or the apex of the arc) is the Connect Groups. I mentioned that many of our parishioners who have gone into the hospital have been lavished with love and prayers from their Connect Group members. I declared, "If you want the church to care for you, then join a Connect Group." And so she did.

When I first arrived at Saint Benedict, I assumed we were asking too much of parishioners when it came to Connect Groups. I have come to discover that they are in fact meeting a desperate need, in that they offer a place for meaningful Christian community.

What do I want you to do?

I have heard all kinds of objections to Connect Groups, most of which have crossed my own mind. Our home could never fit all those people, everyone is already way too busy, and so on. It is true that embracing this model is not easy and will take considerable investment, especially at the outset. However, if your parish is serious about evangelization, you need to come up with a plan to ensure that ongoing discipleship continues after a person has had an initial encounter with Jesus.

Rather than beginning with the obstacles, I invite pastors to sit down with their leadership teams to paint the dream. What would it look like to share the responsibility of pastoring the flock with other capable lay shepherds? If the Connect Group model doesn't work for you, talk about another way to foster small Christian communities so you can be sure that the newly evangelized will be cared for and will eventually become missionary disciples.

CHAPTER 27

A Rewarding RCIA

Usually during the Easter Octave, I suffer the effects of a chocolate egg overdose. At this time of year, I try to revive the back-and-forth proclamation that I learned as a child from Fr. Bob Bedard. He probably learned it from members of Madonna House, the lay apostolate founded in rural Ontario by Catherine Doherty, and her husband, Eddie. Catherine was a Russian baroness, and Madonna House is a beautiful mixture of the Christian East and West.

To begin, the first person exclaims, "Christ is risen!" The response is "Truly he is risen!" The first person continues by saying, "As he said he would." Together, all joyfully shout, "Alleluia!" For me, this dialogue is more meaningful than the trite "Happy Easter," which is repeated hundreds of times as parishioners exit the building on Resurrection Sunday. But whatever words you prefer, we have much to celebrate during Easter, not the least of which would be our new Catholics.

In my first year at Saint Benedict Parish, we were blessed to have a dozen people in our RCIA process, with five of them receiving baptism. I have heard RCIA called the Rite of Christian *Information* for Adults rather than its true name, Rite of Christian *Initiation* of Adults. A common tendency is for those leading the program to drown participants in information. This communicates that our highest priority as a Church is intellectual knowledge.

In some cutting-edge parishes, the facilitators make an effort to foster relationships. Thus the catechumens and candidates grow to appreciate the regular support of small community. But after the Easter Vigil, they are cut loose to blend into the large "community" that gathers for Sunday Mass—during which the highest expression of community might be a meaningful handshake at the Sign of Peace.

As with most things related to Divine Renovation, our RCIA process begins very intentionally with Alpha. In many RCIA programs, Jesus is a "topic" that gets covered in chapter two, after God and before the Holy Spirit, the Church, Mary, and so forth. Sadly, learning to relate to the person of Jesus gets lost somewhere in the pile of Catholic information.

In our case, we deliberately evangelize using Alpha to make sure that Jesus remains front and center—the Alpha and the Omega, as it were. We continue with Catholicism 201 (a video series produced by Fr. James), which helps to fill in basic Catholic-specific content. Even so, we recognize that discipleship is a lifelong journey of growing, learning, and loving. All are encouraged to join Connect Groups to ensure that they will receive post-Easter support in their faith journey.

As he did every year, on Holy Saturday morning Fr. James met with the RCIA group and their sponsors. This was one of his favorite moments of the year. After a time of prayer, the catechumens and candidates went around the room sharing their personal stories. Many tears were shed. Fr. James continued with a reflection on the parable of the sower (see Matthew 13). Not all of the seed was going to survive and produce fruit. After nineteen years of priesthood, he knew that statistically, each of them had a 50/50 chance of still being here in twelve months. He begged them not to delay in taking the next step by joining a Connect Group or a Discipleship Group and getting involved in a ministry.

That night during his homily, Fr. James said, "I testify to you [the congregation] that Jesus has changed the lives of these men and women!" I happily agreed.

What do I want you to know?

Recently I was at a gathering when someone mentioned that a dozen people had just joined the Catholic Church at Saint Benedict. One woman asked, "Are they all getting married to Catholics?" The presumption was that people traditionally swap sides to appease a future spouse or future in-laws. I thought about it for a minute and realized that none of our RCIA group was going through the paces as part of a premarriage rite. God willing, one or two marriages will come about from this group, but I would say that marriage was not the driving motivator.

Jesus rose from the dead and conquered death itself. He continues to reveal himself to people, forgive them, and save them, and he desires to be in relationship with them. Jesus is the reason for this Easter Season, and he needs to be the reason we bring people through the RCIA process into the Catholic Church.

What do I want you to do?

Plan to meet with your RCIA team soon after Easter to debrief with them. In addition to tweaking the mechanics, take an honest look at the principles that are driving your RCIA process.

Have you focused almost exclusively on conveying information? Have you given the catechumens and candidates a taste of authentic Christian community, only to take it away once they have been fully initiated? Do you have a model in place that gives people a high probability of encountering Jesus before they receive the sacraments?

Improve the process for next year so that your newest and most vulnerable members will be set up for long-term success—as disciples of Jesus in the Catholic Church.

CHAPTER 28

Baptism Prep: Epic Fail (Part 1 of 2)

Generally I stick to activities where I know I can win, even though I am told that we can learn more from our mistakes than from our successes. The saints also speak of the rapid spiritual growth that can take place during times of desolation and not just times of consolation. (Consolation is the *feeling* of God's nearness, and desolation is when God *feels* distant.) In my experience, moments of failure can lead to two possible outcomes.

As a seminarian, I once played chess against a nine-year-old boy who had me in checkmate in a matter of minutes. I have had little interest in the game ever since. On the other hand, I can vividly remember failing the motorcycle road test. I was shocked and on the verge of tears as the examiner walked away. Nevertheless, I got back in the saddle, practiced, and passed it the second time around.

Upon arriving at Saint Benedict, I was asked (read: "voluntold") to be in charge of baptism preparation and RCIA. Naturally, this would be in addition to my regular priestly duties. While the RCIA group required a chunk of my time, it was manageable and even enjoyable. Conversely, the baptism preparation process was a grind. As you know, a huge percentage of those seeking baptism for their children have little or no connection to the parish or to God. Our goal is to increase the "sticky-factor" with these people who are knocking on our doors.

There have been a couple of different iterations of baptism preparation over the last few years. These have produced some fruit but have been far from ideal. Many of the team members who were involved in previous attempts became frustrated and disappointed. Some even stepped down before I arrived. There were about seven sets of parents on the ministry team, many of whom found it too time-consuming given the needs of their own families.

As I met with team members and collected data, I tried to craft a new process that would be more sustainable for the team while maintaining a relational flavor. We want new families to feel extremely welcome at our parish, as they interact with other YRPs (Young Relatable Parents—my acronym). The hope would be for the YRPs to share their stories and, in turn, to challenge these new (unchurched or lukewarm) parents to take the next step on their faith journey.

It all sounded great on paper, but as the months went by, it felt like one step forward and two steps back. It was almost impossible to find a time when the whole team could meet. We had to work around schedules, not least of which was nap time (not mine, in case you are wondering). On the F.A.C.T. scale—Faithful, Available, Contagious, Teachable—the team consisted of amazing, faithful young parents, but the "A" was limited because of their state in life. We went from thirteen parents on the team to three. These are some of the reasons the team dwindled: personal reasons, feeling too old, moving, health situations. And once, when we scheduled a meeting, one of the remaining moms went into labor that day! You can't make this stuff up. After all of our efforts, the whole thing was in need of a complete reboot.

What do I want you to know?

My attempt at innovating baptism preparation felt like an exercise in futility. The young team members that I had gotten to know were wonderful people. They would have much to share with those who approach the parish seeking the sacraments. But there was a gap between where I had hoped we were going as a team and where we actually ended up.

Taking risks and trying new things means we might fail on occasion. Through failure, I have learned a lot (I will get more specific in my next reflection).

What do I want you to do?

Sometimes the hardest thing to do is to allow a ministry to die if it is not working. After all, our Christian faith is rooted in the mystery that after death comes new life.

Several months before all this started, I could have single-handedly come up with a plan for baptism preparation and implemented it on my own, perhaps with the help of one other person. This has been standard procedure for me in the past, and it has worked adequately. As Ron Huntley and I discussed my failure to launch this ministry team, the question arose: Would a solo attempt have been sustainable, scalable, and transferable? No, no, and no. Would it have gotten the job done? Yes. So often in parishes, we resort to using people and approaches that get stuff done. In the long run, this only leads to frustration, volunteer fatigue, and burnout.

Do not perpetuate short-term ministry fixes as if they were long-term solutions. It's better to let the thing die before it kills you and your best people.

CHAPTER 29

Baptism Prep: Epic Fail (Part 2 of 2)

Recently, in Confession, one of my brother priests recommended that I reflect on the Garden of Gethsemane. It is easy to judge the apostles for sleeping at the hour of need, but the same phrase often applies to my life: "The spirit indeed is willing, but the flesh is weak" (Mark 14:38). Furthermore, as I continued to reflect on our baptism preparation process, I could see that although there were good intentions on all sides, we had little to show for it. The following are a few of the things I learned from this experience.

First, I recognize my own need for growth in time and energy management. Since I am constantly juggling a variety of responsibilities, it is easy to let one fall by the wayside. Trying to innovate a new way of doing baptism preparation is tantamount to running a start-up company, something that requires a lot of energy and investment at the front end. Everyone was waiting on me to initiate the meetings and the plan. Thus, every time I was traveling or going through a busy season, nothing much happened. In reading the book *Crucial Conversations*—which I highly recommend and write about at length in chapter 48—I also realized that I did not offer enough clarity around expectations. The authors suggest that a team needs to settle the questions of *who* does *what* by *when*, and *how* will you follow up?

Though I need to own the above, some of the responsibility falls on the Senior Leadership Team (SLT). There are always going to be challenging ministries and needs, but I think it was unrealistic for me to have been given this task so early on. Saint

Benedict has never been successful in this particular area; at best we have seen 30 percent of the unchurched get connected through our baptism process. That number is relatively high by Catholic standards, and it is largely because many families have gone elsewhere, decreasing our overall number of baptisms.

It took me a good six months just to get to know some of the key players and to pick up the pieces from the previous failed attempt—by this point, we were attempting baptism prep version 3.0. I was left to work with a ministry team that consisted almost entirely of young parents, with young kids, who were only somewhat in the Saint Benedict Game Plan. We have not had much success in fully engaging this demographic.

But some of the onus is on the team members themselves. The pressures of our world have changed drastically in the last few decades, and I believe young parents are doing their best to respond. On the flip side, as a child I cannot remember a time when my parents were not in some kind of ministry. In fact, they were often leading multiple ministries! Yet today, many parents in their twenties, thirties, and forties are so overwhelmed by the responsibilities of the domestic church that involvement in other ministries is an afterthought.

As a celibate who has never had to stay up all night with a sick child, I am not passing any judgment whatsoever. I am merely making an observation. Perhaps it was naïve to try to build a team made up of parents who were going through this challenging season of life. Ron Huntley likes to quote a friend who asks people, "What would be *easy lifting* for you?" Based on my experience, either this was not a good fit because it's *heavy* lifting, or these parents can help out but should not be expected to lead this ministry.

What do I want you to know?

This may sound provocative, but as a Catholic priest faithful to the magisterium, I've come to believe that dispensing sacraments is too often seen as the mission of the Church. Sacramental preparation can be an opportunity to invite people to take a next step on their faith journey, but, make no mistake, the mission of Jesus Christ is to make disciples! Very often when people come into relationship with Jesus, they will naturally hunger for sacraments—not as milestone events but as spiritual lifelines.

It has been a frustrating experience trying to build this team, but I learned about my own weaknesses, about the way that a leadership team can presume too much of an individual, and about the understandable limitations of parents with young children.

In the words of author John Maxwell, "Fail early, fail often, but always fail forward."

What do I want you to do?

As priests and lay leaders, think of a ministry that you have tried to develop or invigorate that has not gone as you had hoped. Come up with a list of things you have learned from that experience. Instead of blaming others first, always start by pointing the finger at yourself to see how you could have done things differently.

After you have failed and learned whatever you can from the experience, try, try again! It is back to the old drawing board or, in my case, the old whiteboard.

CHAPTER 30

Baby Steps

The decision to allow the old way of doing baptism prep to die and to radically reboot our process has borne great fruit. We hit the reset button and have since managed to get a few key people "on the bus" and sitting in the correct seats. A couple of the new team members are committed and personable and have experienced powerful conversions in the last few years. Their witness is ideal, since most of the parents who bring their children for baptism have been away from the faith. So far we have had two sessions with a total of a dozen families. After a ten-minute personal witness, we break into small groups for discussion. I have been amazed by the openness of the participants. A few tears have been shed as people admit that they have been away from their Catholic faith but are making the decision to reconnect.

As Fr. Rob Arsenault, a brother priest and an avid sailor, would say, "There's been a sea change." As a result, I am feeling reenergized and have been able to focus more creatively on the baptism team. The big challenge now is not just to offer a welcoming and hospitable environment to the parents seeking baptism but, also, to call them to something more. You might remember the classic Bill Murray comedy *What About Bob?* in which the psychiatrist is promoting his new book *Baby Steps*. In our case, the infants to be baptized are not responsible for a faith response, but we do want to help their parents take a baby step in faith. At the end of this chapter is a one-page document we handed out after our third session. After that, team members met face-to-face with each family to discuss the impact of this process on them. We then invited the parents to choose how they wished to respond.

What do I want you to know?

To slow down the sacramental drive-thru, which bears very little fruit in the long run, we try to make it clear early on that we are asking something of these parents. If we expect too much of them all at once, it will either crush them or cause them to be turned off. Hence, in our post-modern world, one tactic is to give the parents the opportunity to choose the particular way in which they will commit.

What do I want you to do?

If your first attempts have been unsuccessful in assembling the right ministry team, don't give up. After reading the document below, think about your own shallow-water entry points. Compile a simple document that could be useful for those running sacramental preparation at your parish. In offering a short menu of choices, you make it easier for those returning to the Church to take a baby step.

"Next Steps" at Saint Benedict Parish

We believe that each one of us is called to be on a spiritual journey, and what matters is not *where* a person is on that journey but that he or she is actually *on* the journey. We welcome all people regardless of the stage of their spiritual life, their struggles, or their past. With that said, every single one of us can take a "next step" in the right direction. The journey we are on is exciting, but it is far from finished. With this in mind, the Bible offers us this simple suggestion: "Draw near to God and he will draw near to you" (James 4:8).

Whether you have been journeying at Saint Benedict Parish for a long time or you have just joined us recently, we would like you to consider taking a concrete "next step." Below is a list of a few possible options. They are not presented in a sequential order; however, the top few make more sense earlier on, and the bottom few would be more appropriate a bit later on the journey. We look forward to discussing in person the "next step(s)" that resonates most with you.

Alpha: We hope that every single person who walks through our doors will try Alpha. This experience involves three parts: we share a meal, we listen to a relevant speaker, and then we have a discussion in small groups, where all are free to engage as they feel comfortable. It is a relaxed and fun way to talk about the most important questions: Why am I here? What is the meaning of life? Is there a God? and so on.

Sunday Worship (Mass): We really make an effort to make our Sunday experience welcoming and fulfilling. Worshipping as a community every Sunday is something that God asks of us. The more we do it, the more we come to appreciate the importance of having this sacred time built into our week.

PACT (Preparing and Celebrating Together): This is a program designed for families with elementary-age children who are preparing for First Reconciliation and First Holy Communion. It takes place on one Sunday each month after the 9 a.m. Mass. There are age-appropriate activities for the children, and the parents are able to participate and learn alongside.

Reconciliation: For many adult Catholics, it has been years since they have been to Reconciliation (Confession). Even though it can be intimidating to confess one's sins to Jesus before a priest, many who muster up the courage to do so find the experience to be nonjudgmental and truly freeing.

Men's Leadership GYM (God, You and Me): This group of men meets for fellowship, inspiration, and prayer every Friday from 6:45 to 8:00 a.m. All men are welcome to attend and be supported as leaders at home, in church, and in the workplace.

Life's Healing Choices: None of us have it all together. We all have stuff to deal with from our pasts. This small-group program offers freedom from hurts, hang-ups, and habits through eight healing choices. True happiness is yours if you are willing to accept it.

SaintBP Serve: Serving in ministry is a core part of what it means to live out the Christian life. We would love to match you with a ministry that will engage your God-given talents and passions so that you can be used to make a difference in our parish and in the world. The more we give, the more we receive.

Discipleship Groups: These small groups of about four to ten people meet for a set time throughout the year (say, four to ten weeks) and are focused on growing in their understanding of the Catholic faith, such as through a Bible study. The groups may follow a DVD series or a book.

Stick with the Plan

Nerf guns have become a necessity at our Senior Leadership Team (SLT) meetings, and they reveal something of our culture. Our meetings are both intense and fun! Patrick Lencioni, the best-selling author on organizational health, has made the observation that most people are happy to sit through a two-hour movie that has little or no bearing on their lives but are bored out of their minds in an equally long meeting. In the movie, we get caught up in the conflict, and so it is not boring. If the meeting is boring, it is because we do not actively participate—and we fail to speak about the things that matter. There is a high level of trust and healthy conflict among our SLT, which allows for interesting and "dangerous" meetings.

Initially I found these meetings difficult and exhausting, but I have come to see their value. Fr. James reminded me of one of the first SLT meetings in which I participated. The discussion got heated at one point, and so he looked over at me to make sure that I was okay. I guess my complexion must have been slightly paler than normal. Over time, I have been able to bring more things to the table and have gotten better at vocalizing my honest opinions.

Many months ago, I had to say no to a parishioner who made a request that did not need my direct involvement as priest. A few weeks ago, I found myself in a similar but different scenario when someone from outside the parish approached me. This married layman is about my age and zealous for the kingdom, and he has developed a new apostolate focused on evangelization. I love what this organization is doing! In fact, I have had a few opportunities in the past to do ministry alongside them, and it has always been an easy fit, loads of fun, and very fruitful. So you can imagine my excitement when he proposed a kind of partnership with our parish. Still, from the beginning, part of me hesitated. We have already developed a clear and focused model, and this would mean embracing a second ministry model, which also happens to be well thought out and mission oriented.

When the discussion came up at our SLT meeting, everyone quickly confirmed my hunch. We all love this organization and are united in the same vision of bringing people to Jesus in the power of the Holy Spirit. However, it would not make sense to try to mesh these two slightly different strategies. From our perspective, we need to stick to the Saint Benedict Game Plan.

This experience also taught me another lesson about team dynamics. People process information and arrive at decisions at various speeds. Fr. James and Ron Huntley have probably been the fastest in our group. Kate Robinson, who always has profound insights, usually needs a bit more time to ponder and reflect. My guess is that Rob McDowell and I are somewhere in the middle.

In the midst of it, the others could see that I was still wrestling with having to say no to this brother in the vineyard. The team did not leave me hanging but insisted that I try to express my concerns. In the end, it was just a question of my needing a little more processing time. Intellectually I knew it was the correct way to go, but I still had to struggle with it emotionally.

What do I want you to know?

After the meeting, Fr. James jokingly said, "Now you know how I feel." He is constantly approached by great people with incredible ministries who have a desire to partner. I was amazed to hear some of the household names in the Catholic world that he has had to turn down, not the least of which was EWTN.

After our conversation, Fr. James tweeted the following: "Saying NO to bad ideas is easy. Saying NO to good ideas is difficult but often necessary if a church is going to be intentional and focused." The alternative is for your parish to end up like Bilbo Baggins from the Lord of the Rings, who eloquently said, "I feel thin, sort of stretched, like butter scraped over too much bread."

What do I want you to do?

I may sound like a broken record, but it is so important to clarify the vision. What is the future picture of your parish that excites you? Formulate a strategy to start moving people in that direction. When those things become more obvious, you can courageously say no to all the other good ideas that do not align themselves with the vision and strategy of your parish.

Priests need to establish teams of lay people around themselves who understand the vision and strategy and who can hold them accountable. Do you have a culture where the people around the table feel comfortable about keeping the leader focused? If not, it is the priest's responsibility to help the other team members feel safe enough to express their opinions.

Also, don't forget to be attentive to the unique persons on your team, some of whom might need more time to process information. Their contributions are equally valuable.

Leadership Development

Parish transformation will remain a hypothetical theory without clear and consistent leadership. I would summarize the Divine Renovation model as follows: first you need to live—not just talk about—certain values as a parish (Fr. James suggests ten in his book); these will lay the groundwork for a healthy culture; healthy things grow and bear fruit; the greatest fruit will be a church full of missionary disciples ready to transform the world.

However, the cultural inertia to remain stagnant in maintenance mode is powerful. We have to keep our "hand to the plow" and continually nurture the kinds of cultural values consistent with a vision of a missionary community. Likewise, no game plan is ever perfect in concept or execution. Therefore, in order to sustain parish renewal beyond its initial appearance, we must raise up and equip new generations of leaders who understand the principles behind our shared culture, bold vision, and pastoral strategy.

In many ways, leadership development—that is, calling forth and preparing leaders—is one of the most central tasks of parish renewal. In the following reflections, I break open some of the key lessons I've been learning at Saint Benedict regarding how to develop leaders and about the importance of self-leadership.

CHAPTER 32

Multiplication Mindset (Part 1 of 2)

A few years ago, I was chatting with an engineer who told me that he used to work as a self-employed consultant. He soon discovered that there were a limited number of hours in a week for which he could bill clients. This capped his income. Eventually he felt prompted by God to build an engineering business. The business grew quickly, and he was soon employing a few dozen people, including some members of his parish. Not only was he using his intelligence and gifts to put bread on the table for his own family, but he was also helping to support dozens of families—because he was able to look beyond his personal abilities.

Within a few weeks of my arrival at Saint Benedict, I could see that the staff was very intentional about leadership. This means that the priests and staff do not do all the work—they raise up others to join in Jesus' mission. These, in turn, are called to apprentice others. As a result, many more lives are touched. This has led me to ponder a few things I learned from my earlier work as a campus chaplain at Wayne State. (The next reflection will focus more on the parish.)

I first heard about spiritual multiplication—as opposed to spiritual addition—from Catholic Christian Outreach, a Canadian university movement. I have since heard FOCUS (Fellowship of Catholic University Students, based in the United States) give a similar presentation on the topic. I suspect they both borrowed the idea from Campus Crusade for Christ. Here's how it works: if one very gifted evangelist (say, a priest) converted 1,000 people every day through his preaching, it would take him almost 20,000 years to reach the whole planet. But if a multiplier disciple invested in one person for a year, and the next year they both invested in one new person, and in the third year the four multiplier disciples each invested in a new person, the Gospel would reach the ends of the earth in under thirty-seven years! (I think the math is correct; maybe I should verify it with that engineer.)

As I got to know the students on campus, three stood out as being superstars. After they had fully encountered Jesus in the power of the Holy Spirit, they were willing—and had the capacity—to do just about anything for the kingdom. There were ten to fifteen other students who were also evangelized and committed to the cause. I invested a great deal of time in this small group, and soon we were working together to reach others. As a brother priest, Fr. Allan MacDonald, likes to say, I was loitering with intent.

My deepest desire is for everyone to experience God's love for them because I know this has the power to change lives. Over the years, I have found that praying with people so that their hearts would be filled with the Holy Spirit (see Romans 5:5) is one of the simplest ways to bring this about. While in Detroit, I was on the lookout for opportunities to pray with people. If I met someone who seemed open to being prayed over, I would ask their permission to invite a few other students to join us. I usually began by sharing a simple Gospel message and a brief version of my own testimony. Then I would ask if it was okay if we laid hands on the person as we prayed that they would be filled with the Holy Spirit. Again, our goal was for them to experience genuine love from us and from God.

After a while, the student leaders followed my example and became comfortable sharing, guiding the prayer, and even listening for an inspired word from the Spirit. Without thinking about it, I was modeling a simple approach to evangelization that was touching people's lives. These young adults continued to pray with others, in this way, long after I left Detroit.

What do I want you to know?

The Catholic world is set up for spiritual addition, not spiritual multiplication. Everything goes straight to the priest and is expected to come directly from him. If we continue with an addition-only approach, we will limit the number of lives that can be transformed.

The way that a celibate priest can bear the most fruit is through shifting his mindset to think in terms of spiritual multiplication—raising up others to join in the mission.

What do I want you to do?

Jesus had an inner circle of three disciples and a group of twelve apostles. Make a list of the best people in your parish in whom you could invest and who could eventually do some of the ministry you do.

For lay leaders, if your priest is going to multiply himself in you, you will need to be ready to free up time, to walk alongside him, and to allow him to pour his heart into yours.

CHAPTER 33

Multiplication Mindset (Part 2 of 2)

could never be like Fr. James Mallon!" This is a common refrain from priests who hear about the success of Saint Benedict Parish. The majority of Catholic parishes are failing miserably, and yet the Divine Renovation model seems too intimidating. Some say that the only explanation for the fruitful results is that this is a unique situation built around a personality cult.

Being of Indian descent, I have no desire to become the Brown Fr. James. Personality, gifts, and quirks aside, I believe we need to multiply the parish renewal innovations that God has been bringing about at Saint Benedict—that includes the way we operate as priests. No priest should try to become like someone else, other than Jesus. As Matthew Kelly would say, "I am striving to become the best version of myself." But the best version of me cannot stop with me! Unless I figure out a way to multiply myself, when I leave—and eventually die—so will all the great ministry I have been spearheading.

At Saint Benedict, there is a desire to keep spiritual multiplication on the radar at all times. The staff is constantly building teams of leaders around them who are in turn building other teams of people engaged in ministry. For example, our hope was to serve meals during Alpha this fall rather than do it potluck style. We want to make it as easy as possible for our guests. A parishioner stepped forward, offering to cook all the meals for Alpha! This man has some time on his hands, is very capable, and has a wonderful personality. Any parish would dream of having such a committed volunteer. So you can understand that I was taken aback when a staff member stated firmly, "He will not be *allowed* to do this by himself. We expect him to create a team of people who can help out in the kitchen." In other words, though he could probably operate solo, that is not an option for us. Part of his responsibility is to build up others in the gifts of service and hospitality.

One morning over my first cup of coffee, I had a conversation with Fr. Rob Arsenault, a brother priest. He had been doing some amazing work fostering the Companions of the Cross Lay Associates in Halifax (these are lay people who share in my religious community's vision and spirituality). His basic approach is to spend time with people, get to know their stories, and lead them lovingly into a relationship with Jesus. Without a doubt, he is incredibly gifted with people and there is plenty of fruit to show for it. So I asked him, "How can we multiply Fr. Rob?" In other words, what if we had a small army of lay people—I would settle for a dozen—who were on the lookout to invest in people, get to know their stories, and love them into friendship with Jesus? Imagine the impact that that could have on a parish community.

Begin with your strengths. If a priest is gifted in hospitality and encouragement, he should equip others to do the same as a form of pre-evangelization—a way to build trust. If a priest is a powerful preacher or teacher, it is his responsibility to coach others to become amazing communicators (both ordained and lay). If a priest is a ridiculously good administrator, I would love to work with him. Seriously, though, he should be developing teams of lay people who love to organize and urging them to organize parish events for the sake of the kingdom.

What do I want you to know?

I can say, from firsthand experience, that the success of Divine Renovation is not due to the person of Fr. James Mallon—quite the opposite. No priest should feel pressured to become like him; we need to be ourselves. But we can imitate Fr. James' example of inviting and equipping the saints (gifted lay people) to share in the renewal of the parish (cf. Ephesians 4:12).

Spiritual multiplication is about leaving a legacy—not in things but in people who know your mind and your heart. If you have a burning desire to lead people to Jesus, this needs to be passed on to others so the mission will continue long after you are gone.

What do I want you to do?

Saint Paul models spiritual multiplication in the New Testament. Spend some time in prayer with 2 Timothy 2:2: "What you [Timothy] have heard from me [Paul] before many witnesses [through other intermediaries] entrust to faithful men [those you invest in] who will be able to teach others also [so the multiplication will continue]."

Start thinking in terms of working yourself out of a job. This applies to both priests and lay leaders. What are the areas in your ministry where you are passionate and where God has uniquely blessed you? Keep an eye out for people who have the capacity to be excellent in those areas, and start to invest in them so they can apprentice others.

CHAPTER 34

Nouning the Verb "Ask"

F r. Bob Bedard, the founder of my community, was a high school English teacher for almost twenty years and a master of the language. On more than one occasion, he made a point of correcting my mistakes in English. Now it is my turn to make a grammatical observation concerning the parlance around the parish, specifically the morphing of the word *ask* from verb to noun. It has become commonplace at Saint Benedict and in Christian leadership lingo to throw around phrases like "That's a big ask!" or "Who is going to make the ask?" Speaking in this manner adds a certain *gravitas* to situations when we must step out of our comfort zones to make a financial appeal, to call people to serve in ministry, or to present the Gospel in a way that elicits a total giving over of one's life to Jesus.

As usual, I was inspired by a homily at our recent Companions of the Cross retreat. It is not enough to talk about fishing or even to be a recreational fisherman. A priest has to become a "livelihood fisherman" who can show the fruit—a freezer full of fish—as evidence of his efforts and God's blessing. When it comes to evangelization, priests need to lead by example.

When I moved to Nova Scotia, I discovered that I have a distant relative living nearby. We connected and decided to go out for dinner on her birthday. It was wonderful to be able to catch up. In many ways, we were getting to know each other for the first time. I happened to take a little Alpha pamphlet along with me, suspecting that she was no longer a regular churchgoer. I was a little nervous about inviting her out of the blue, because

I had not taken the time to invest in our relationship. Amazingly, we talked and talked for hours, and she began asking all kinds of faith-related questions. She seemed very open. At the end of the evening, I pulled out the pamphlet and said something like, "It was awesome sharing a meal together. You're so easy to talk to. I would like you to consider coming to this course at our church called Alpha. Since you are friendly and outgoing, I think you'd love it. It's actually really fun . . . not that different from what we did this evening. We get together for dinner and have a great conversation." She was open to the possibility but said she would have to talk it over with her husband, who is also away from church.

I shared the story later at a staff meeting. Ron caught me doing something well and affirmed it. Ron speaks of leaders being in one of four quadrants:

- Unconscious Incompetent (not good at something and unaware of it)
- Conscious Incompetent (aware of a weakness and teachable—a good place to be)
- Unconscious Competent (me, in that situation, unaware of why I was effective)
- Conscious Competent (aware of what works and able to transfer principles to another)

He really liked the way I made the ask, focusing on her gifts and how she would love Alpha, instead of presenting it as an imposition or a demand. I didn't even realize what I had done but was grateful that he was able to identify the tack I had taken.

(Please note that I have learned and applied these "Four Stages of Competence" in a slightly different order than normal. For the purpose of this example, it seemed to make sense to leave them in this sequence. See the Resources section for more information online.)

What do I want you to know?

Priests are constantly in situations where they must make difficult requests of others: for more money, for more volunteers, for more people to make the decision to surrender their lives wholesale to Jesus, and so on. Learning how to make an effective ask is something that will serve you well in a variety of circumstances.

When it comes to inviting the unchurched to evangelization opportunities like Alpha, leaders have to be willing to make the faith "ask." We can't just expect our people to invite their friends and family because we tell them they should.

What do I want you to do?

Identify the things that you feel most uncomfortable asking for. Determine which of these you *need* to ask for anyway, as a priest. Find a "solve" for some of the other big requests that need to be made. For example, delegate a much more competent and confident layperson to make a financial appeal, if that is an area that you find challenging.

Bonus (for priests and laity): Catch someone doing something well this week and affirm them. Be specific in your affirmation in order to help them become more conscious of their competencies.

CHAPTER 35

Getting a Personal Trainer

At the beginning of 2016, I decided to do the most cliché thing imaginable: I got a gym membership. Regular physical fitness has always been part of my life. In my early days in seminary, I had a membership at the RA Centre in Ottawa. Fr. Bob Bedard was a long-time member at this fitness club. He shed so much sweat on those cardio machines that they might become second-class relics one day. The hot tub at the RA Centre is already an unofficial pilgrimage site. Regarding gym fees, I have tried my best to avoid paying money for self-inflicted torture. But I had been spoiled by so much East Coast and East Indian hospitality that I needed to act quickly before I turned into a samosa.

When it comes to exercise, I have no interest in pairing up with a personal trainer. I can be disciplined when I want to be, and I have a fair degree of experience with working out. But when it comes to a lot of other areas in my life, I could definitely benefit from a bit of one-on-one coaching. I have greatly appreciated the parish renewal and leadership coaching I have received from a few key people at Saint Benedict. I have also had the opportunity to spend some time coaching a couple of deacons and priests in the area of preaching. Gifted individuals have poured time and experience into me, and I have tried to pass it on.

In my opinion, the fastest way for priests and lay people to improve as leaders is for us to develop a culture of coaching in the Catholic Church. We need conferences and big visions to inspire us, but the day-to-day implementation will require something else. The great thing about coaching is that it happens in real time. As you work through an issue, you can bounce ideas off a mentor and get immediate feedback. Big projects can be broken down into bite-sized steps. A good coach will help you identify areas of weakness and keep you accountable to your goals. Ultimately, he or she will enable you to excel in your strengths.

Around the same time that I got the gym membership, Ron Huntley and I went to a Halifax Mooseheads hockey game. His son, Christian, has played as a defenseman in the same league for the Quebec City Remparts. Naturally, Ron and I got talking about hockey—as gentlemen do. Over the years, Christian has been blessed to play under some fantastic coaches. At one point, Ron asked his son to name his favorite coach. Without hesitating, Christian responded, "Dad, when I played for Coach Dean, somehow I was always able to find another gear. He helped me to play at my best!"

What do I want you to know?

Receiving personal mentoring from someone with a little more experience and wisdom has been invaluable to me. I need someone I respect and trust who can speak into my life, encourage me when I am down, and challenge me toward greatness.

In January of 2016, we received another priest at Saint Benedict who was beginning a six-month Divine Renovation internship. Much of the research speaks of the 10/20/70 rule. In other words, 10 percent of learning happens at big conferences, from talks, and from reading books. The next 20 percent comes from hands-on experience (sitting in on meetings, participating in ministries, and so on). The final 70 percent takes place when you go home and try to implement what you have received. Principles are quickly forgotten without ongoing support and accountability once a leader returns home and is inundated with the busyness of parish life. Hence the learning agreement we established with Fr. Michael Leclerc (and the Archdiocese of Montreal) included having him remain in a coaching relationship with us after leaving our parish. This ongoing personal training has set him up for success in his own context.

Because of the incredible response to the book *Divine Renovation*, the Divine Renovation Ministry has established the Divine Renovation Network (DRN) to offer coaching to priests and parish leadership teams that are motivated to learn.

What do I want you to do?

Let me first ask you this question: Who is coaching you right now in regard to leadership?

Whether you are a seminarian, a young priest, a pastor, a layperson on staff, or a lay volunteer, you need someone you can look up to and who can push you to keep growing. As it says in the Bible, "If you love to listen you will gain knowledge, / and if you incline your ear you will become wise. . . . If you see an intelligent man, visit him early; / let your foot wear out his doorstep" (Sirach 6:33, 36).

Whether it's the New Year or not, make a resolution to find a personal trainer (coach/mentor) who will help you become a better leader.

CHAPTER 36

Calling All Leaders

My first year of seminary formation took place in Combermere, a rural part of Ontario, where I was able to do a lot of hiking and snowshoeing. It was a great way to encounter God through his gift of creation. There is nothing quite like climbing to the top of a huge hill and enjoying the panorama from the summit. I had many memorable moments of sheer solitude from a glorious lookout. I have also enjoyed leading groups of seminarians, friends, and family members to a few of these special places. Interestingly, Jesus did a lot of his most significant work from high places, not the least of which was Mount Calvary.

For more than twenty years now, Bill Hybels and Willow Creek have gathered people together to experience the Global Leadership Summit (GLS). People of all stripes and faiths unite annually to grow in leadership skills. Some travel to Chicago to experience it live, and others watch from one of many video host sites worldwide. The impact on religious and secular leaders has been immeasurable. But why wait twelve months for the next GLS?

Leadership is an ongoing reality that requires regular inspiration and equipping. Thus we invite the key leaders from all of our ministries to gather at least three times during the year for a local parish Leadership Summit. I was really looking forward to our Summit in January 2016, which would be my first. It was a highlight for me to be growing alongside approximately one hundred of our best lay leaders at the parish.

Let me explain the structure of our three-hour Leadership Summit. As with most things at the parish, there was hospitality—coffee, tea, and finger foods—to welcome people as they arrived. We wanted to honor the sacrifice of their time on a Saturday morning, so the schedule was jam-packed, fun, and interactive. After an opening prayer and introduction, we played an icebreaker game at our tables.

Ron Huntley followed this with a review of the three Critical Success Factors (CSF) that apply to any ministry. We all need to strive to build a healthy rather than a toxic culture. He invited me to share about our recent liturgical changes, which were poorly communicated by the Clergy Team and therefore opened up a portal for gossip, complaining, and all-round negativity. We have to fight against human nature and always be vigilant, choosing health over toxicity!

Second, Ron spoke about our apprenticeship culture. Every person in leadership needs to be on the lookout for a person to mentor. He used the image of King Saul riding into town after battle and only receiving a fraction of the attention David received upon his later arrival. This led to jealousy and Saul's eventual demise. Things would have been different if King Saul had chosen to share his chariot with David. By riding in together, Saul would have communicated the following message: "Look, everyone, this is my number-one general whom I have been raising up to take over when I am gone. We should all be proud of him."

Finally, every ministry was encouraged to develop a leadership pipeline with an easy entry point for parishioners to begin serving. As they become more experienced and trustworthy, they can be given more and more responsibility and authority.

This is the leadership pipeline that the Hospitality Ministry created: Taking up the Collection > Greeter > Usher > Hospitality Lead at a particular Mass > Hospitality Lead overseeing the entire Ministry. We don't want people to stay in the same ministry forever, essentially clogging the pipe. By moving people through the pipeline, we can grow our parishioners and make room for new people to begin serving in little ways.

What do I want you to know?

Leadership development is at the core of Divine Renovation. It is beneficial to invite key leaders up to a summit from time to time, to help them regain perspective. Personally investing in them as leaders helps them to grow and makes them feel appreciated. This is a venue where we can revisit the vision and present key leadership principles that can then be shared with the people in their respective ministries.

What do I want you to do?

What events do you have in place that bring all the parish ministry leaders together? As a leadership team, brainstorm ways to make these gatherings more engaging in order to increase their "value-for-time." Think of one or two things you would want all of the leaders at your parish to know (and to do). Share these at your next gathering of parish leaders.

CHAPTER 37

Elevator Pitch

This might sound like the beginning of a bad joke, but what do summits and elevators have in common? For one thing, they are both about getting to great heights. Referencing Vatican II (*Lumen Gentium*, 11), Sherry Weddell of the Catherine of Siena Institute has spoken about the Eucharist as the "source and summit" and remarked, "Anyone who lives in the mountains knows that you don't just arrive at a summit! It takes a lot of hard work to get there." Many of us would probably prefer to just step into an elevator, push a button, and ascend to the top. To use this analogy, it will take effort (read: leadership) and a lot of grace from "on high" to move a parish to the place where the celebration of the Eucharist is truly a summit experience.

In my previous reflection, I described the first segment of our parish Leadership Summit, which involved a review of the three Critical Success Factors. At the end of the gathering, Fr. James spoke to the leaders, reviewing some of the parish history, the vision, and the big-picture strategy. I enjoyed the entire Leadership Summit, but it was the middle section that I found most interesting and interactive.

One of the problems facing any ministry leader is finding volunteers. Ron Huntley reminded us to get in touch with our "White Hot Why." This is not so much about what a particular ministry does but why it is vital. Then he gave us a few minutes to draft what is commonly referred to as an elevator pitch. In other words, what would you convey to someone if you had only about 60 seconds with them? Ron said that the following four elements are essential in an elevator pitch: grab their attention, identify the problem, present a solution, and make the ask.

Since I am the "bus driver" (lingo to suggest that I am in charge) of the baptism preparation team, I decided to create a 60-second script to invite someone to join our team. It went something like this: "The other day I had a chance to hold a newborn in my arms. Don't you love babies? I'm convinced that parents love their children and want to do the best for them. Many parents bring their babies to get them baptized at our church because they believe it's the right thing to do. Sadly, about 80 percent of them have little or no connection to our parish. After their child is baptized, about 80 percent of the families are still not connected with our parish. We've been missing a huge opportunity here. In response to this, a group of us is trying to innovate a new baptism process that would be fun, hospitable, and also challenging—to invite families to take the next step in their faith journey. I think you would be an incredible addition to our team. Would you consider helping us to reach those babies and their parents?"

After our crowd of one hundred leaders drafted their elevator pitches, we paired up and had a minute to deliver our pitch before switching partners. It was kind of like speed dating (not that I would know). Everyone had a chance to deliver their elevator pitch three or four times, modifying and improving it with each attempt. The whole experience was hilarious, awkward, and effective. Afterwards, one woman shared that a recruiter from the Knights of Columbus had delivered his elevator pitch in a very convincing manner. She wanted to know where she could sign up.

What do I want you to know?

Developing and rehearsing an elevator pitch is a fun way to help clarify and improve the core message of a particular "ask."

In his previous career, Ron worked in sales. He used to train with one of his fellow salesmen before going out to potential buyers. Practice makes perfect! Rob reminded us at the Leadership Summit that we often hear stories of military personnel or those in first responder situations who say, "I didn't know what to do—then my training kicked in." That is the reason why we should practice.

What do I want you to do?

As a priest, identify a ministry that needs more people to step up and serve. Create an elevator pitch incorporating the four key elements. Practice it and then try it out.

Better still, gather a group of lay leaders and teach them how to hone their skills so they can help to close the deal. The day after the Leadership Summit, I had a meeting with the young adults who were to give witness talks as part of the new baptism preparation process. We did a speed-dating elevator pitch exercise together as a group. It was definitely outside of their comfort zone, but I know it helped me, and I think it helped them to refine their main message.

CHAPTER 38

Playing to Your Strengths

One of the permanent deacons at Saint Benedict invited me to play soccer at a friendly kick-around once a week. I was huffing and puffing on the bench between shifts when the guy next to me asked me my age. I told him that I was thirty-four and then asked his age. He was seventy-two! It is a little humbling to admit that the U-75 league is a good fit for me, but it is a fantastic group of guys. A few days ago, the coach of the men's national soccer team played with us, which is kind of a big deal. I guess it would be an even bigger deal if Canada were to ever qualify for the World Cup. In any case, I know that I can run faster and longer than most people twice my age—no surprise there—but if I am not clear about what position I am playing or where I am best suited, it can end up being a lot of work with few results.

The importance of strength-based ministry is not a new concept. Many will already be familiar with the idea of working from their spiritual gifts. I have used and would recommend the gifts inventory developed by Sherry Weddell and the Catherine of Siena Institute. Spiritual gifts are found in the early Church—see 1 Corinthians 12, where the Church is also described as the Body of Christ made up of many members who have complementary gifts, all for the common good. In a parish, where the needs are never-ending, we generally look to fill holes rather than proactively help our parishioners to serve where they are most passionate, where they will be most satisfied. By the way, gifts and strengths are not to be pitted against each other. If your gifts look to *what* God is calling you to, your strengths zero in on *how* you will tend to do it.

As well as the ME[25] survey discussed in previous chapters, Saint Benedict has embraced another Gallup tool, the Clifton Strengths Finder. In addition to the staff, over three hundred parishioners have taken this thirty-minute online survey to help pinpoint their top five "talent themes" (from a list of thirty-four). This has helped individuals to grow in self-knowledge and to appreciate the different strengths that others have. In fact, only one in 275,000 people will have the same top five talent themes!

In Winseman, Clifton, and Liesveld's book *Living Your Strengths*, a *strength* is defined as "the ability to provide consistent, near-perfect performance in a given activity. This ability is a powerful, productive combination of talent, skill, and knowledge" (p. 7). A *talent* naturally exists within you and is said to be a recurring pattern of thought, feeling, or behavior; it is instinctive. A *skill* is the ability to move through steps in a task and can be acquired through practice. *Knowledge* (what you know) can also be learned through study or training.

For example, a person with "Competition" (one of Fr. James' top five) will have the same basic thought/feeling/behavior whether on the soccer field, in a classroom, or driving parish renewal. However, the skills and knowledge needed for success in each unique situation will vary drastically. Normally, in a Christian context we would consider something like "Competition" to be negative, prideful, and self-centered (that is, sinful). Yet a person wired this way—recognizing this as a positive talent—can be freed up to develop skills and knowledge in this area to turn it into a productive strength while also recognizing its potential pitfalls.

What do I want you to know?

Priests and lay people alike are more engaged and more productive when they can work out of their strengths. When I discovered that "Achiever" was one of my top talent themes, it came as a relief. In the past, I almost felt as if I had to apologize for having a "big engine" to get stuff done. For this to grow into a full-fledged strength, I still need to submit it completely to God's redeeming power and not let it drive me around frantically.

You may prefer to rely solely on a spiritual gifts inventory or some other self-knowledge tool such as the temperaments, Myers-Briggs, or DISC. Whatever you choose, you need to find a common language to help staff and volunteers understand themselves and each other. It will also help connect them to appropriate ministries.

What do I want you to do?

Speaking of gifts, this might be a good time to ask Santa to put the book *Living Your Strengths (Catholic Edition)* under the tree for you this year. The book includes one Clifton Strengths Finder code allowing you to complete the online survey. Or you can go directly to their website and pay the nominal fee, currently $20, to take the survey (see the Resources section). You are given only about twenty seconds to answer each question, so set aside thirty minutes of uninterrupted time to complete it.

If you begin to incorporate the Strengths Finder culture at your parish, you might also want to start assembling well-rounded teams according to the particular strengths of the individual members. I have noticed that both the Senior Leadership Team and the Clergy Team at Saint Benedict have a balanced representation of the four main strength categories: Executing, Influencing, Relationship Building, and Strategic Thinking.

Refer to *Divine Renovation Guidebook* for more on the strengths and for a chart laying out the thirty-four talent themes according to these four categories (pp. 22–23).

CHAPTER 39

Learning to Say No

When I was first ordained, in addition to being an associate pastor at a busy parish, I was the chaplain of the Challenge Movement, the youth version of Cursillo. I was running around to youth and young adult events hosted by the National Evangelization Teams (NET) and Catholic Christian Outreach (CCO). I was meeting with a handful of spiritual directees, and my dinner calendar was booked months in advance. Needless to say, I have always had trouble saying no. I went to a brother, Fr. Galen Bank, for Confession during this phase, and he gave me the following penance: say no to the next ten requests that come across your desk. It was one of the hardest penances I have ever done, but I believe it was inspired, and it gave me a taste of pastoral sanity.

Many of us priests care about people and try to be generous—even sacrificial—with our time. In truth, I have often said yes because saying no leaves me feeling a bit like of a failure. It is humbling to recognize my limitations and to admit that there are some things I am simply unable to do.

Moving to a new place and into a new assignment offers a clean slate and an opportunity to learn from previous mistakes. Within a couple of days of my arrival at Saint Benedict, a parishioner asked me to be the spiritual advisor for their ministry. As I understand it, the previous associate pastor had attended all of their monthly meetings. I knew that I would regret taking this on once the ministry year got under way. What's more, there was already a structure in place whereby the ministries report to the Pastoral Leadership Team (PLT), which was led by Ron Huntley, and ultimately to the Senior Leadership Team (SLT). I was able to send a message via our office manager, graciously declining the request and offering a few reasons why. It was a small victory for me!

I shared the incident later at a PLT meeting, where I was affirmed for not saying yes to that scenario. Ron also challenged me to try to understand "the why" in the future. Why did this person think they needed a priest (me) to be directly involved in their ministry? While the occasional technical or theological question might arise, chances are that one or more people in the group had a solid faith foundation. God has certainly put a passion in their hearts for this ministry, and he wants to build them up to be leaders. In other words, by not understanding and responding to that "why," I missed an opportunity to turn a request that required a no into a moment to empower the laity.

Fr. James is not very good at saying no either—he and I seem to share a few of the same weaknesses. He regularly receives requests to speak at conferences all over the world, to take on new projects, to create new multimedia resources, and so on. Most of these arrive through Fr. James' personal assistant, Anne Marie Sime, who triages them and has to decline the majority right off the bat. When he was the pastor of Saint Benedict, he would submit the requests that seemed reasonable to the SLT. Together, the five of us would talk about whether this "ask" would fit into the grand scheme of where God is leading us as a parish. If Fr. James had to have an uncomfortable conversation by responding with a no, he could use the SLT as a scapegoat. He brought the request to the team, we gave it serious consideration, but collectively decided to turn it down.

What do I want you to know?

Every priest is limited to 168 hours in a given week and can easily get busy doing things that fill the time. We need to say no to the many "good things" that are being requested of us so that we will have the time and energy to say yes to the "God things" that he is asking of us. Saying no is not easy, but the good news is that you don't have to do it alone.

What do I want you to do?

If you are not good at saying no, develop a system or a process that will assist you. First, it might help to slow down the requests. If people are looking for an answer on the spot, a priest should not feel pressured to respond to their urgency. It might be useful to say that you are going to bring the request to a weekly leadership meeting. Even requests that seem small will take a portion of a priest's time and energy and could divert him from the things he needs to stay focused on.

If you are already good at saying no to people, look for ways to turn each no into an opportunity to positively empower lay people to become leaders in their own right.

For lay leaders, this is one of those areas where priests need your support and need you to keep them accountable: to let their yes be yes and their no be no. Even Fr. James tried to sneak a few things by us every once in a while. As the SLT, it was our responsibility to help him to stay firm in saying no to the things that take him away from the main thing.

CHAPTER 40

Haters Gonna Hate

Chances are that if you are out front, leading with innovation, sooner or later you will get arrows in your back (or your butt . . . or both). Priests know this to be true. I am sure all of us have a quiver full of stories of nasty complainers. One of the most "impressive" critiques, which I received years ago, was from someone who did not appreciate that my preaching was so joyful. They went to the trouble of creating an anonymous e-mail account (something like fromafriend@ hotmail.com) to share their concerns with me. They even sent me video links from an extremely right-wing media personality to prove that joy distracts us from orthodox Catholicism. (I had to pull out the dictionary a few times to make sense of this expert's vast vocabulary.)

Looking back, I can laugh about these e-mails, but at the time this criticism really bothered me. I continue to pray for more of the fruits of the Holy Spirit to be manifest in my life— love, joy, peace, patience, and so forth (see Galatians 5:22-23).

Recently, after preaching about Jesus' response to the man to "go, sell what you have, and give to the poor" (Mark 10:21), I was accosted by a woman who had a theological disagreement with me. As she saw it, Jesus was in no way suggesting that we need to be financially generous. Instead, he was asking us to give a little of our time. Furthermore, she insisted that she knew a lot of very nice rich people. Ultimately, I think she was just annoyed that I had the audacity to talk about money at church, no doubt spoiling her Thanksgiving weekend.

I can't say that I enjoy that kind of contrary energy coming at me, and, after the fact, I usually think of better ways I could have responded. But as I reflected on the encounter, I laughed to myself when I realized that *only* one person complained. As it turns out, she was a random visitor. Kudos to Fr. James and the team for creating a culture at Saint Benedict whereby money is a part of the normal discourse. (After all, it was a topic that Jesus spoke of often.)

Keenly aware that criticism is something that I find difficult to deal with—it can easily deflate me—I brought it up in one of my first one-on-one meetings with Fr. James. I asked, "How do you deal with criticism?" His response: "Not very well." That being said, he has improved considerably in this area from when he was first ordained. He has developed a kind of flow chart to filter through the plethora of complaints that come in:

- If the administrative assistant receives an anonymous letter, she shreds it without even telling Fr. James that it came in.

- If a person is quick to criticize but is not united with the parish vision and has made little effort to participate in the overall parish strategy, then a polite "thank you" is in order. This person's comments are not given any serious thought.

- If a parishioner is on board with the vision, is invested in the strategy, and has some suggestions to offer, perhaps with regard to a particular tactical (rather than strategic) approach, that person deserves some attention. Fr. James might sit down with them to hear the concern. They might offer legitimate ideas that are worthy of consideration and implementation.

What do I want you to know?

Expect pushback! This is especially the case if we are trying to lead our parishes to a place where they are impacting both the members on the inside and the people on the outside. Newton's Law of Inertia comes into play: objects at rest like to stay at rest. The same can be said of dormant Catholics.

What do I want you to do?

We all need to brace ourselves and develop a thick skin when it comes to negativity. Don't allow yourself to take all of these criticisms personally. We must rediscover our deepest identity as sons and daughters of a Father who loves us. I suggest praying with the story of the baptism of Jesus in the Jordan (Mark 1:11). Let those words of God the Father wash over you: "You are my beloved; with you I am well pleased" (New American Bible).

Priests need to strategize with their frontline staff or volunteers to develop a basic approach for dealing with complaints. To properly discern if a person's criticism is worth your time, the leadership team must clarify the vision. I hope that every Catholic parish sees itself as a place where missionary disciples are formed. If a critic is fully in line with this vision and its respective strategy, then be open to receiving their insights with humility.

(For more on dealing with negativity and pushback, see *Divine Renovation Guidebook*, pp. 67–69.)

CHAPTER 41

Big MAC Attack

I generally try to avoid fast food, but there is nothing like fasting on Ash Wednesday to make me crave a Big Mac. Those first few days of Lent are especially tough with the added Friday fast forty-eight hours later. I picture the Thursday after Ash Wednesday as a kind of juicy burger sandwiched between two "bread days." Be sure to enjoy it!

In any case, MAC also stands for the Mid-Atlantic Congress, which I attended in Baltimore, Maryland, in 2016. Fr. James Mallon and I traveled to this gathering of about 1,500 Catholics from the region. He was asked to lead a special track for about one hundred pastors and their leadership teams. I appreciated the opportunity to get a refresher on the central themes of *Divine Renovation*. Fr. James also led the group through a few exercises to help them develop vision and look at their teams in terms of their strengths.

One highlight for me was walking by a table that was doing an exercise on trust and healthy conflict—based on Patrick Lencioni's materials (he is also one of the founders of Amazing Parish—see the Resources section). The men on staff, including the pastor, thought they were doing just fine when it came to healthy communication. The women did not feel the same way. The secretary felt that she was low on the totem pole and, as a result, could not share her honest opinions on key issues. The pastor was surprised by this revelation, as he had always tried to make everyone feel equal. We talked more about how they could create a safe environment among their staff, and I had the opportunity to pray with them afterwards. I believe they experienced some healing through that conversation.

Later Fr. James led the entire group through a prayer exercise—in huddles of three or four people—inviting them to give thanks, to intercede, and to pray over each other. He walked them through a simple step-by-step process that turned out to be quite powerful for the different teams.

Fr. James returned home after the two-day conference, while I stayed on for the weekend to visit the Church of the Nativity in Timonium (the home of *Rebuilt*). Fr. Michael White and the staff of about two dozen received me graciously. They allowed me to see what was going on behind the scenes, to sit in on a few meetings, and to ask a bunch of questions. Having experienced a few Masses there and encountered several parishioners, I am convinced that their innovations are faithfully Catholic.

About 4,000 people go through their doors every weekend, and hundreds are involved in ministry of some kind. They have iPads set up at the exits of the church to make it as easy as possible for people to sign up for their "Next Steps." STEPS is an acronym for Serve, Tithe, Engage in Small Groups, Practice (Prayer and Sacraments), and Share (Evangelization). For example, a person can choose to try a "First Serve," where they are plugged into a ministry to have a one-off taste of serving without any long-term commitment.

On a different note, their tech and in-house video production is light years ahead of anything I have ever seen in a Catholic church. Ultimately, it was their dynamic children's ministry that left me with the greatest sense of "holy envy." Close to a dozen rooms are occupied by different age groups during the weekend Masses. They use this opportunity to instill a culture of service and small groups from a young age.

What do I want you to know?

I mentioned to Fr. Michael White and his staff that it is not uncommon for people to approach us at Saint Benedict and say things like, "I prefer *Divine Renovation* over the book *Rebuilt*." Our standard response is that we are all on the same side, and we're excited to see different models of church renewal develop. In fact, we admire what they are doing at Nativity and recognize that in some areas they are several "steps" ahead of us. It is wonderful to have friends in the Catholic world who share the same heart and who are taking risks as they implement new ideas. Their crisp mission statement says it all: "Love God. Love Others. Make Disciples."

As with my visit to Holy Trinity Brompton in London, I was filled with inspiration as I saw another working incarnational model of what is possible when a church orients itself toward mission.

What do I want you to do?

We can all get stuck in our own circumstances of hopelessness, believing that this is the way things will always be. Just as I received much from visiting Nativity, the pastors and leadership teams benefited by participating in the Divine Renovation sessions during the Mid-Atlantic Congress.

I encourage you to make plans to visit a church that is innovating (or to attend a conference) to broaden your scope of the grander vision that God has for his Church.

Finally, priests and their teams of lay leaders must have honest conversations about healthy conflict. Due to the power differential, pastors can assume that things are fine when they may not be. Third-party mediators are sometimes needed to help a team get to a deeper place of vulnerability-based trust.

Refer to *Divine Renovation Guidebook* (pp. 28–34) for a helpful team exercise.

CHAPTER 42

A Little Change Is a Big Change

When I first arrived at Saint Benedict, I noticed a couple of things about the way Mass was celebrated that were different from what I had seen elsewhere. You could say that I was coming in with fresh eyes and "rookie smarts" (to use a term I heard at the 2015 Global Leadership Summit). Most of what I saw were wonderful innovations geared toward helping people connect with each other and God.

After a couple of months, I suggested a few minor "altarations" at one of our clergy meetings, specifically to help streamline what we were doing at the altar. For example, Holy Communion is always offered under both species, so there are at least four ciboria and four chalices (and the equivalent number of extraordinary ministers of Holy Communion) at every weekday Mass. There are even more on the weekends! We were using a gigantic bowl-shaped ciborium at the Sunday Masses, which was probably intended to reserve consecrated hosts on Holy Thursday. I was thinking about starting a rigorous exercise routine so that I would have the strength to lift this large ciborium at the Great Doxology.

What made matters worse was trying to divide the consecrated hosts from the big one into six smaller ciboria in a timely fashion during the *Agnus Dei*, without scattering sacred particles everywhere. (If you are unfamiliar with this churchy liturgical lingo, please don't worry. The point is that some tweaks were in order.)

After some discussion, the clergy team agreed to most of my ideas, and we delegated the responsibility of communicating the changes. No big deal, right? When I got back from a couple of weeks of vacation in India, I heard a lot of parishioners chattering about how overwhelmed they felt by *all* of the *big* upcoming changes at Saint Benedict. These were scheduled to take effect the First Sunday of Advent—the beginning of the new liturgical year. When I dug a little deeper, I learned that an e-mail—which was heavy on details and technical language—had gone out to over three hundred parishioners involved in liturgical ministries. Many were caught off guard, confused, and feeling as if they had not been consulted.

As an example, our streamlined process involved using a tray to carry several ciboria up the aisle during the Offertory. This became a source of incredible anxiety. One person was shocked that we would jeopardize the lives of "good Catholics" by making them walk up the sanctuary steps carrying this heavy, ungodly tray. Another person even had trouble sleeping! Would these changes impact the premium on our parish insurance policy?

I am being a little facetious, but to be honest, I was blindsided by the pushback, negativity, and resistance to these slight adjustments. All of these comments were symptomatic of the fact that we had done a poor job of handling the change.

What do I want you to know?

Leadership is about moving a group of people from one place to another place. This will inevitably involve change. Rob McDowell, our Director of Parish Life, pointed out that there is a difference between "Change Leadership" (leaders need to have the guts to see and communicate what has to be changed) and "Change Management" (how you go about implementing the change—making it as easy as possible for people to get behind you).

Even though these liturgical tweaks had nothing to do with our eternal salvation or the mission of the Church, for many people even a small change can feel like a really big change.

What do I want you to do?

Be sensitive to the people you are leading and try not to make the same mistakes I made. If I could do it again, I would clarify the "why" behind the change. I would gather a small group of leaders of the various liturgical ministries and articulate this "why" to them—possibly using the "From Here to There" approach, painting a picture of the future and explaining why staying here is not an option. I would present the basic idea and get their input to arrive at the best possible solution. Then I would give the ministry leaders hands-on training and ask them to train their teams. Finally, I would make sure there was plenty of time to roll out these changes.

Ron Huntley often reminds me that Holy Trinity Brompton, where the Alpha process was created, models the following principle: when things go well, the leader deflects the praise; but when things go south, the leader takes ownership for the mistakes, not scapegoating someone who had been delegated a task. This was one of many instances when I had to apologize first before we could continue onward.

CHAPTER 43

If Moses Supposes
(aka Leading Transition)

The English rhyme from 1896 begins: "If Moses supposes his toeses are roses, then Moses supposes erroneously." After all, he did spend a lot of time in the desert. Then again, perhaps this biblical hero was still in "de-Nile." However, one thing that Moses did grasp was how to effectively move an entire community through transition.

I am grateful to Brett Powell, a gifted lay leader in the Catholic Church in Canada, who shared a classic essay with me by William Bridges: "Getting Them through the Wilderness: A Leader's Guide to Transition." The following is a brief summary of some of the key points.

Most leaders, whether in the Church or the business world, confuse the concepts of change and transition. Bridges explains: "Change is situational . . . the shift in the strategy. . . the switch in reporting relationships. . . . Transition, on the other hand, is a three-phase psychological reorientation process that people go through when they are coming to terms with change."

You might think of change as the objective realities that need to be modified for an organization to be healthy and effective. As one example, priests and church staff in the 21st century have had to adjust their ministry in response to the invention of e-mail. But transition deals with the subjective shift that needs to take place within the person. And so, for example, it might be difficult for some parishioners to let go of their tangible envelopes and stamps in order to switch to electronic mail, which is faster and usually more reliable. Keep in mind that it's one thing to tell people that we need to change, and it's another thing to actually lead them through a period of transition.

The Old Testament story of the Exodus highlights these three phases of transition. First, an organization needs to "leave Egypt," letting go of their previous reality and identity. As Bridges says, "Unless people can make a real ending, they will be unable to make a successful beginning." The second phase of "wandering through the desert" in the neutral zone is a necessary and dangerous time. It is a time both for old behaviors and attitudes to die out and for creativity and innovation. After walking through those first two phases, it is then possible for an organization to "enter the Promised Land" with a new sense of energy and purpose.

So often churches are "in bondage" to an old way of doing things that worked in a bygone era. Perhaps a parish has grown beyond a seat-of-the-pants management style, or there is too much complex bureaucracy given its current smaller size. If as leader I make the case to "let my people go," the initial response (like that of Pharaoh) is for parishioners to tighten their grip on the old system. Sometimes financial problems, reduced Mass attendance, or a clergy shortage (plagues) can be blessings in disguise, forcing the people to realize that the status quo (staying in Egypt) is not an option. But a group can't simply arrive at the Promised Land because they decide to leave Egypt. Moses used the crossing of the Red Sea as a "boundary event" to make a clear distinction between leaving phase one and entering phase two. While making a clean break, always speak respectfully of the past and honor the people who served during that period. They helped to bring the organization to where it is today.

Before reaching the Promised Land, it is important to spend an adequate amount of time in the desert (phase two). Similar to the Israelite lamentations for garlic and leeks back in Egypt, people tend to react to the neutral zone by idealizing the past. These might be common sentiments expressed over coffee and donuts after Mass:

- "What was so bad about Egypt (the way things used to be) anyway?"
- "Do you think Moses (Father) really knows where he's going?"
- "I'd never have left if I had known it was going to take this long!" (Or for Catholics who own vehicles, "I'd have gone to Mass elsewhere if I had known . . . ")

Moses used a couple of different strategies in the desert. First, he showed the people some quick successes (such as the manna and quail) and celebrated them. Second, he resisted the temptation to short-circuit the pilgrimage, even though a few scouts had set foot in the Promised Land early on. They could not complete the journey until those who had known Egypt had all died. Symbolically, the attitudes and behaviors from the old way of doing things need to completely die out.

What do I want you to know?

William Bridges says this:

> We see change as something akin to crossing the street—something that is dangerous to do slowly.

> Many leaders fail to realize the importance of managing transition, believing that if the structural, technical, or financial changes go well, the human transitions will take care of themselves.

Catholic parishes need pastors and leadership teams who, like Moses, can patiently help the community to recognize these three phases and journey through them. It's worth it to transition to a future land flowing with milk and honey . . . and disciples!

What do I want you to do?

If you have not yet come across this leadership classic, "Getting Them through the Wilderness: A Leader's Guide to Transition," it is a must-read (see the Resources section).

Carefully work through this essay as a team. Identify some of your past failures to transition parishioners through change. Decide on how to practically apply some of this wisdom to bring about future and lasting cultural changes at your parish.

CHAPTER 44

Dynamic Downtime

E veryone wants a happy priest!" I remember one of my brother Companions making this statement some years ago. If memory serves correctly, it was said tongue-in-cheek as a way to justify more time for sun, sand, surf, and recreational hobbies. Parishioners expect their pastors to be present, hardworking, kindhearted, and men of prayer. Still, if we were to poll the folks in the pews, my guess is that ten out of ten would also want their priests to be healthy. Physical, mental, emotional, and spiritual health is closely connected to happiness.

Anyone who knows me will see the hypocrisy in my pontificating on the subject of balance and self-leadership. Full disclosure: I tend to live dangerously close to the red zone, so I write this as a neophyte and not as an expert. As it stands, we are already feeling the pinch in the province of Nova Scotia, with fewer and fewer priests on hand. Hence, those who are active in ministry—and interested in working for the renewal of the Church—need to take good care of themselves. They also need to make sure that their lay leaders are able to get the rest they require.

Many experienced priests will recognize that there are lulls in the liturgical year that allow for moments of respite: July–August, pre-Advent, post-Christmas, post-Easter. The question is whether we "put money in the bank" when we have the chance. Do we plan periodic rest and take it guilt-free?

I am used to being busy, but by mid-February of my first year at Saint Benedict, I was peaking. I had missed a couple of days off in a row because of work-related travel and our Parish mission. Many expectations, some internally motivated, were pulling me in multiple directions. When I am overwhelmed, I am often blindsided by my emotional vulnerability. Thus, an unexpected request for an Anointing of the Sick felt like the straw that broke the camel's back. Instead of compassion, I gave in to anger and self-pity.

When I was able to step back from the situation, I discovered that something needed to change. In fact, some things had changed! For example, after Christmas, Alpha moved from Friday nights to Thursday nights. That subtle difference caused me to do a double commute (a total of eighty minutes in the car) an extra day each week. This also meant that I lost an evening that had been earmarked for creative work, such as homily preparation. I used to think that if I could just master the formula for a balanced life, I would be able to go into cruise control. As it turns out, there are many moving pieces in our lives, so we have to be flexible and dynamic in our pursuit of balance. It became clear that I needed to build more margin into my life. After talking to Fr. James and Ron, they agreed that I could block off one morning a week to work from home. Having that time away from the office created a new window for creativity and gave me a chance to catch up with fewer distractions.

What do I want you to know?

As priests who are in leadership positions, we should begin by leading ourselves so that we are operating out of a place of peace, joy, and energy. Growing in self-knowledge is key to understanding what we *need* to be healthy. Once those things become clear, we have to be committed to finding ongoing balance in our lives as circumstances and expectations shift around us.

As it turns out, people really do need their priests to be happy and healthy.

What do I want you to do?

Watch Wayne Cordeiro's talk "Dead Leader Running" from the 2006 Global Leadership Summit (see the Resources section). Cordeiro shares his own journey of almost pushing to the point of no return. He reminds church leaders, "We don't forget that we're pastors. We forget that we're human." His challenge—and my challenge to you—was to make a list of "What fills your tank?" and "What drains your tank?" We will be able to face draining situations if we are pouring in good things that fill us up. Prayer, sports, exercise, reading, and dinners with friends are nonnegotiables for me. What is on your list?

Some priests who are really good at protecting their own time can unknowingly leave their staff and key volunteers to wilt on the vine. After a busy season like Christmas or Holy Week, be sure to check in with your best people and insist that they take a few days to recuperate, especially if they think they are too busy. It might help if you shut down the office for a few days or reduce office hours.

CHAPTER 45

Paying It Forward

You might remember the film *Pay It Forward*. In this movie, a teacher challenged his class to think of a way to change the world and put it into action. Our typical response toward a good deed is to pay back the person with an equivalent act of charity. Instead, one boy decided he would change the world by showing kindness to three new people, encouraging each of them to continue to pay it forward. It is not hard to see the mission of Jesus Christ in this simple model.

In June of 2016, Saint Benedict hosted over six hundred delegates from at least eleven countries for the Divine Renovation (DR16) conference. It was a highlight to have thirty of my Companion brother priests join, learning about parish renewal firsthand at an incarnational conference. If I could summarize DR16, I would say that our primary goal was to pay it forward.

By that time, Fr. James, the staff, and the parishioners had been riding a wave of grace from the Holy Spirit that was undergirded by healthy leadership practices. I refuse to believe that God would only desire renewal for one pastor in one particular context. DR16 was about sharing what we have received so that others can also be blessed. In fact, Ron Huntley said in a debriefing afterwards that we will have real credibility when some of the other parishes represented at the conference start to get healthy, grow, and bear the fruit of changed lives.

Paying it forward can happen on a large scale, but often it is done person-to-person. In the lead-up to DR16, many of us were frantically developing our workshops. I started formulating an outline for my "Sunday Experience" workshop (or the three *H*s—hospitality, hymns, homilies) six weeks beforehand. As Ron and I whiteboarded a few ideas, he helped me understand that I needed to identify the gap. It was not enough to convey a few good ideas (best practices) that people could borrow to tweak their Masses. Rather, I had to communicate the "why" behind embracing change. Given his coaching, I gave my workshop an overhaul to connect more urgently with Jesus' mission.

Prior to DR16, I delivered my "Sunday Experience" workshop at an Archdiocesan Assembly. I was also able to sit in on Kate Robinson's presentation at the Assembly, which was a dry run for the one she would present during DR16. Far be it from me to offer our Director of Communications advice on how to more effectively communicate, but I suppose that is what happened. To put it differently, I tried to pay it forward. Using some of the concepts Ron shared with me for developing a strong presentation, I helped Kate to whiteboard an improved structure that would cover her core content in a way that was more interactive and engaging for the crowd.

Around this time, the Operations Team was rehearsing its panel discussion for DR16. I sat in and fired difficult questions at them about office administration, finances, and facilities. They later paid it forward, passing on their wisdom to the conference delegates.

What do I want you to know?

It is common knowledge that we learn the most when we try to teach others. That being said, I am not sure if this is common practice in Catholic parishes. At times, parishes and pastors who are doing something effective will turn inward, as if to protect the recipe for their secret sauce. This is symptomatic of a Church that, as Pope Francis has observed, has become self-referential.

We are all on the same team! When I learn something new that works, it should be automatic for me to want to pass it on so that others can benefit—provided they wish to grow. When they succeed, I am able to share in their joy.

What do I want you to do?

I was chatting with a friend—a DR16 delegate who is involved at Our Lady of Good Counsel Parish in Michigan—who suggested that everyone should have three mentor relationships. We need to seek the wisdom of elders who are ahead of us on the journey. We also need the encouragement of peers who are working through comparable challenges. Finally, we all need to be raising up others. Do you have each of these relationships?

Identify two or three people in that third category to whom you can pay it forward. Think of a way you can concretely pass on your learning to these individuals. You might need to begin by asking their permission to offer some coaching. For example, I asked Kate if I could give her feedback on her presentation. She was incredibly open to my input—she is far humbler than I am. Make it clear that your objective is to help them reach the best of their ability.

CHAPTER 46

Under the Hood

A few months ago, I noticed that my car had started making new noises. Given my limited expertise when it comes to auto mechanics, my first solution was to crank the music louder. When the noise began to overpower the radio, I decided to visit a parishioner who has a reputation for being an "engine whisperer." He opened the hood and noticed a heat shield that had come loose and was rattling around, and so he tied it down properly. But as I drove away, the din continued. Thankfully, I have a good friend who is a retired mechanic—and a prayerful disciple. I left my car with him for a few weeks. He had to lift the engine right out of the frame in order to rebuild the transmission. The point is that the repairs began when someone took a look to see what was going on under the hood.

The 2016 Divine Renovation conference (DR16) was intense but very satisfying. There were so many graces from the amazing talks and testimonies, powerful moments of worship and prayer ministry, and opportunities for networking between sessions. Among the many highlights was the Tuesday morning tag-team plenary given by Fr. James and Ron Huntley (see the Resources section). It was a fun and vulnerable exposition of what goes on behind closed doors at Saint Benedict. Our six hundred guests from around the world discovered that "renovating divinely" has not been easy. As recently as two years earlier, the parish was in a very unhealthy place. Fr. James was traveling and speaking around the world, the parish was growing, and the staff was suffering. Worse still, Fr. James was not fully aware of the problems.

Everyone needed to start paying attention to the noise under the hood. The journey toward healing and health was one that required vulnerability. Fr. James needed to apologize for his own mistakes. Taking the advice of a consultant (Brent Dolfo), he was encouraged to call a team of people around him to assist him with leadership. It was at this point that he made the shift from "leading a team" to "leading out of a team." This was the beginning of the Senior Leadership Team (SLT). Creating a safe space for healthy conflict at this leadership level has been the secret for rebuilding the engine at Saint Benedict.

Leading a parish is like owning a FIAT (Fix It Again Tony). There is always repair work to be done, because imperfect and broken people continue to rub up against each other. On the Thursday after DR16, Ron shared with the Companions of the Cross priests about a recent breakdown. He and Jen Ferrier (the former Saint Benedict staff who oversaw Alpha) were set to co-lead an Alpha workshop during the conference. In his excitement, he dominated the conversation and answered almost all of the questions. Afterwards, Jen courageously shared that she felt disappointed and never wanted to do another presentation with him. Ron realized that he had blown it and asked for her forgiveness, hoping that she would give him another chance to regain her trust. The next day, when they gave the same workshop, Ron was more sensitive, and the delegates benefited. As a healthier team, they were once again functioning like a well-oiled machine.

What do I want you to know?

Real leadership requires a great deal of humility and vulnerability. These are qualities that Fr. James had to develop and that have helped him to become a strong pastor. People can smell authenticity and they can tell when you are being fake. The Catholic Church needs leaders who are not afraid to take ownership of their mistakes. It is only then that parishes will come to a place of health, start to grow, and bear fruit.

What do I want you to do?

Get ready to eat a lot of humble pie.

As priests and church leaders, we do not need to go around saying sorry for every little thing—although it would be very Canadian to do so. We do need to be honest and to err on the side of humility. Even if your intentions are good, if others have been hurt by your leadership, it is your responsibility to go to them to start regaining their trust.

If you are sensing there is a problem, you can begin with tentative questions like these:

- "Did I give you the impression that . . . ?"
- "How did you feel when I said . . . ?"
- "Help me to understand the part you are struggling with . . . "

CHAPTER 47

Backroom Deals

F r. Mike Schmitz (of YouTube fame) was in Halifax for the 2016 Steubenville Atlantic youth conference. We were blessed to have him swing by Saint Benedict for a couple of hours that Sunday afternoon. As we took him on a tour of the church, we showed him one of our meeting rooms. Kate Robinson gently pointed out that I had not followed whiteboard etiquette, since I had left some notes up for well over a week. Later I spent a good deal of time cleaning the board with the proper spray and a lot of elbow grease. It occurred to me that if I had just followed the protocol—cleaning things up as soon as possible—it would have been easier for me in the long run.

A little while ago, three members of the Senior Leadership Team (SLT) found themselves in situations where they had to eat humble pie. Various conversations with parishioners began with sincere apologies. With permission from those involved, I will explain how I had to clean up one of the messes I had created.

A wonderful young couple, Sarah and Phil Marmen, lead our Praise & Worship Band at the 9 a.m. Mass on Sundays. I have been getting to know them in recent months, being relatively close in age and sharing a few common interests. Now we find ourselves in the same Connect Group. They asked if I could meet with them to offer guidance on two matters: Phil was preparing to give a Connect Group talk that week, and he and Sarah were planning the Exalt music conference, which would be taking place two months later. I agreed to this ad hoc get-together, and I shared a few thoughts and opinions on both topics.

About forty-eight hours later, I was in an SLT meeting and decided to give the others an FYI that planning was under way for Exalt. I began whiteboarding from memory some of the key elements of the music conference. The SLT suggested a few changes, and I was instructed to follow up. I took a picture of the whiteboard, with a few of the areas in question, e-mailed it to Sarah and Phil, and asked if we could get on a phone call shortly. An hour or so later, I was speaking to Phil, who was a bit taken aback by our questions and feeling as if we were micromanaging them. In fairness, every single Saint Benedict ministry has some level of oversight from the parish leadership. (As it turns out, our little chat uncovered a lack of clarity around the main objective of the event and the target audience.)

By the end of our conversation, I realized that I had made several mistakes. Sending an ambiguous whiteboard picture beforehand—thinking it would save time—caused Sarah and Phil to arrive at certain conclusions that were not accurate. I quickly apologized and reaffirmed that we had total confidence in their abilities.

As I reflected with Kate and Ron the following day, I realized that I had innocently made an even greater error. Unknowingly, as the band leaders approached me to seek my advice, we all broke protocol. In our structure at the time, they should have been supported by our Music Coordinator, Paul Lang, who in turn would report to Kate. If she had any concerns about the conference, she would have brought them up for discussion at our SLT meeting. This accidental workaround was a good opportunity for all of us to learn.

What do I want you to know?

In the military, they speak of breaking the chain of command. This sort of thing happens all the time in parishes. The Praise & Worship Band leaders have a relationship with me on several levels, so it seemed natural for them to seek my advice. They were not deliberately trying to bypass the organizational structure.

However, a priest must be aware of this tendency for parishioners to go straight to the top to get his ear on any number of issues. This clerical approach can also be reinforced when priests go out of their way to make backroom deals with individuals in ministry.

What do I want you to do?

Establish the proper lines of communication and support. Everyone in parish ministry should have someone they can approach with questions or concerns. Once that is in place, priests must not work around the system. If parishioners go directly to the priest, he should receive them warmly and then redirect them to the proper person who can help with that particular issue. When a mistake is made, be quick to correct it and clean up the mess.

CHAPTER 48

Conversing Crucially

S aint Teresa of Avila referred to prayer as an intimate sharing between friends. Much of Scripture can be seen as dialogues between God and humanity. In our modern world, we are constantly in communication, so it should not come as a surprise that parish ministry is filled with these human exchanges.

After taking part in the 2015 Global Leadership Summit at a video host site, we wanted to take a step to grow in our leadership. As a Senior Leadership Team (SLT), we decided to set aside the first thirty minutes of our weekly meetings, over the course of a few months, to work through the chapters of the book *Crucial Conversations*. The following is a basic summary of the key principles.

A conversation is said to go "crucial" when three elements are present: opposing opinions, strong emotions, and high stakes. As humans, we have been conditioned for fight or flight, so when the going gets tough, all the blood flows away from our brains and into our arms and legs. That means we have to recondition ourselves in these crucial moments. Our primary aim should not be to win the argument but to seek understanding. The authors say that dialogue is defined as "the free flow of meaning from two or more people." For this to happen, individuals must have the opportunity to contribute their thoughts to what is called the "Pool of Meaning." For a person to want to share, it is up to the leader to "Make It Safe" to do so.

Leaders should encourage ideas and input from others, even if these might seem controversial at first. Be aware that when we disagree with something we hear, our instinct is to react with Violence or Silence (fight or flight). We will either slam an idea outright or remain mute, fuming inside and later making our thoughts known in unhealthy ways, such as through gossip. Instead, we need to train ourselves to welcome these differing opinions and respond effectively. Even so, our tendency is to avoid certain subjects altogether because we do not want to be forced into one of two options, referred to as the "Fool's Choice." Either I speak the truth or I maintain the relationship. But what if both were possible?

Begin by looking at yourself and not by trying to fix the other. Ask yourself complex questions to get the blood to flow away from your limbs and back into your brain. *What do I really want for myself? What do I really want for others? What do I really want for the relationship?* And finally: *How would I behave if I really wanted these results?* It might be wise to explicitly share that you care about the other's goals and that you respect them as a person (creating Mutual Purpose and Mutual Respect).

Leading up to a crucial conversation, we can often tell ourselves stories about why a person said or did something. The story playing in our head might paint us as the Victim or the other as a Villain. These focus on only a part of the story. Ask yourself this question: *Why would a rational and decent person say or do this?*

Among the many acronyms (memory aids) in the book, to proceed, I should try to "STATE My Path." Share your facts, Tell your story (the conclusions you are starting to form in your head), Ask for the other's paths (listen to their facts and stories), Talk tentatively, and Encourage testing (invite opposing views). If you hope to have a successful dialogue, be sure to remain tentative in your assessment of the situation.

What do I want you to know?

In one of our SLT book-club sessions, someone used the term "critical" conversations by accident. Fr. James referenced the Greek and the Latin to help us understand the etymology of the two words. "Crisis" means a decision point, but the word "crucial" is connected to the root word *crux*—which means "cross." These conversations are always challenging, may involve some suffering, and require truckloads of humility. Yet just as the Cross was necessary prior to the Resurrection, crucial conversations can breathe new life into relationships and situations. I am still a beginner and I make many mistakes, but I have experienced a few of these redemptive conversations.

The above concepts, written in this abbreviated manner, are probably difficult to follow. The thing you need to know is this: A person is not born a conversational expert but can learn and develop this set of skills.

What do I want you to do?

If you have not already done so, read *Crucial Conversations* or listen to the audiobook. After discovering this material, Fr. Rob Arsenault, a priest in my community, has become a great advocate for *Crucial Conversations*. He has used these tools on campus, at the archdiocese, and internally with the Companions of the Cross.

Like many people, I would say that I'm not that good on my feet. But that can become an excuse. Leaders need to practice soft skills to get better at making it safe, resisting the predisposition to fight or flight, talking tentatively, and ultimately, speaking the truth in love. Begin by counting the number of crucial conversations you find yourself in this week.

No Man Is an Island

I have to admit that I have not read Thomas Merton's book *No Man Is an Island*, but I do love the title, which comes from the poem by John Donne. I would argue that "No Priest Is an Island." And if he is, he will have little long-term impact bringing about renewal—especially in the parish context. In the 21st century, the rules of engagement have changed, and the only way forward for the Catholic Church will be through effective team leadership.

I have to admit that my attitude toward playing and working with others has also changed over the years. I grew up enjoying individual sports like swimming, cycling, and snowboarding. When it came to my studies, I often ended up being assigned to group projects where I was the one doing most of the heavy lifting. In high school, by a random series of events, I found myself in student politics. I served (and I do mean *served*) as the co-president of my high school in my final year. The whole experience left a bad taste in my mouth. Surrounded by people who were elected mainly due to popularity, I soon came to the conclusion that "If I want something done, I'll have to do it myself!" It has taken a long time for me to trust that others care as much as I do and that we can work together to achieve success.

Not long ago, I was meeting with my fellow Connect Group leaders. (Our particular group is geared toward twenty- and thirty-somethings.) Many in our group were simultaneously on team for Alpha that season. To make sure we would not let the guests slip through the cracks, I suggested that we invite the people at our young adult Alpha tables to join our Connect Group. I was sure that this was a great idea and would help to boost our numbers, which had dipped since the school year began. I was completely surprised to hear that the other group leaders disagreed with my point of view. Of all the names I mentioned, they did not think that any would be ready to join our Connect Group! As the discussion continued, they emphasized the importance of the paradigm shift from receiving to giving. It would be better for Alpha "grads" to return on the Alpha team so they would get training and be put in situations where they must serve—putting the needs of the guests before their own. Later they would be able to join our Connect Group, not as passive members but as active contributors. I realized that I might be wrong and my co-leaders could be right. On my way home, I happened to visit another Connect Group, which had just ended. I asked those group leaders for their opinion. They agreed wholeheartedly with my fellow leaders.

Not long ago, as a Senior Leadership Team (SLT) we discussed an upcoming Reconciliation Service. In the interest of time, and considering the shortage of priests, I suggested that we skip over the *service* and go directly to the *sacrament*. The other members asked me questions and challenged my desire for efficiency at the expense of the overall experience. This time I went home convinced that I was right and they were wrong. Later I listened to an audio recording of a workshop Fr. James had given on Confession. Something he said in that presentation clicked, and I realized—once again—that the other leaders were right to value the Reconciliation Service as a whole. I went back to the SLT to apologize and withdraw my comments.

What do I want you to know?

Of all the things I have learned and written about from my time at Saint Benedict, my number one takeaway is that I cannot do this alone. Being at the parish and working alongside so many competent leaders has helped to heal a lot of old wounds and hesitations that I had about teamwork. When I work alone—in my inflated estimation—I probably get it right about 80 to 90 percent of the time. But sometimes I get it wrong. When I do get it wrong, I can get it very wrong, and there can be serious consequences. I need a solid group of people around me who can speak honestly into these real-life decisions that will impact real people.

Since writing this chapter, and through God's surprising providence, I have become the pastor of Saint Benedict and am thrilled at the opportunity to lead from within an amazing and gifted leadership team. Aware of my own brokenness and limitations, I cannot even imagine the challenge of becoming a pastor without the support of a strong leadership team. Not only is it more fun, but being part of a good team has helped me become a better priest and a better person.

I somehow managed to avoid reading much Aristotle while in seminary, but I believe he was correct on this point: "The whole is greater than the sum of its parts."

What do I want you to do?

If you are a priest, I urge you to gather three or four lay people around you to help you lead the parish. Patrick Lencioni recently wrote an antidote, in a way, to his earlier book

The Five Dysfunctions of a Team. His new book is titled *The Ideal Team Player.* Ideal team players have three essential virtues. They are Hungry (driven), Humble (coachable) and Smart (this specifically refers to "people smarts" or emotional intelligence). These people exist; we need to discover them and invite them to join an inspiring vision.

In addition to having these three qualities, your best leaders need to love Jesus and love the Catholic Church. They should also have a deep respect and love for the priesthood, without having any desire to become clericalized themselves. Furthermore, these lay leaders must be filled with so much love for the Church and for her priests that they will be unable to sit around and watch as both continue to decline.

If you are one of these passionate lay influencers—willing to commit and take risks for the kingdom—approach your priest with humility and share with him your dream for a future Church, one that is healthy, growing, and bearing fruit.

The good news is that even the best teams are not left to accomplish this mission by human effort alone. As Jesus said to his first leadership team,

All authority in heaven and on earth has been given to me. Go therefore and make disciples of all nations, baptizing them in the name of the Father and of the Son and of the Holy Spirit, teaching them to observe all that I have commanded you; and lo, *I am with you always, to the close of the age.* (Matthew 28:18-20; emphasis mine)

Resources Referenced in Chapters

Introduction Fr. James Mallon, *Divine Renovation: Bringing Your Parish from Maintenance to Mission*
Fr. James Mallon, *Divine Renovation Guidebook: A Step-by-Step Manual for Transforming Your Parish*
divinerenovation.net/renewal_ministries (5 video interviews about DR)
saintbenedict.ca (Saint Benedict—Media, Livestream, Bene Dictus, and more)
companionscross.org (Companions of the Cross—homily podcasts and more)

Chapter 1 Fr. Michael White and Tom Corcoran, *Rebuilt: The Story of a Catholic Parish*
rebuiltparish.com (for more books and parish resources)
churchnativity.com (Church of the Nativity—the home of Rebuilt)

Chapter 3 Matthew Kelly, *The Four Signs of a Dynamic Catholic*
Search for Fr. Mark Goring's daily videos on YouTube.
Fr. Bob Bedard, *We Are Called to Be Companions of the Cross*

Chapter 5 Search for Fr. John Riccardo's podcasts on iTunes.
olgcparish.net (Our Lady of Good Counsel, Plymouth, Michigan)
Fr. Mark Goring, *Treasure in Heaven*

Chapter 6 Fr. James Martin, SJ, *Between Heaven and Mirth*

Chapter 7   Just for laughs, search YouTube for "Michael Jr. How Comedy Works."
Search YouTube for Brian Regan and Jim Gaffigan (two other clean comedians)

Chapter 8   Dale Carnegie, *How to Win Friends & Influence People*

Chapter 9   Search YouTube for the "Saturday Night Live Christmas Mass" skit.

Chapter 10   Nicky Gumbel, *Why Jesus?*

Chapter 11   saintbenedict.ca/treasure2016 (preaching series on giving, Saint Benedict annual financial report—full of personal testimonies and the commitment card)
Robert Morris, *The Blessed Life: Unlocking the Rewards of Generous Giving*

Chapter 12   Fr. Michael White and Tom Corcoran, *Tools for Rebuilding: 75 Really, Really Practical Ways to Make Your Parish Better*
saintbenedict.ca/funerals (articles, slides, audio on changes to funeral process)

Chapter 13   Online search words: "July 25, 2013, Pope Francis Young People Argentina"

Chapter 14   Sherry Weddell, *Forming Intentional Disciples: The Path to Knowing and Following Jesus*

Chapter 16   birkman.com (The Birkman Method)
cco.ca (Catholic Christian Outreach—a Canadian university movement)

Chapter 17 Dave Ferguson, *Keeping Score: How to Know If Your Church Is Winning* downloadable e-book at exponential.org/resource-ebooks/keeping-score.

Chapter 18 Tim Keller, "Leadership and Church Size Dynamics," seniorpastorcentral.com/wp-content/uploads/ sites/2/2016/04/Tim-Keller-Size-Dynamics.pdf

Chapter 19 Albert Winseman, *Growing an Engaged Church* gallup.com/products/174866/faith-member-engagement.aspx (ME[25])
Rick Warren, *The Purpose Driven Church*
Max Depree, *Leadership Is an Art*

Chapter 20 Search YouTube for some Bear Grylls videos, including "My Greatest Adventure"

Chapter 21 Search YouTube for "Bill Hybels Leading from Here to There"
willowcreek.com/events/leadership (Global Leadership Summit)

Chapter 22 livestream.com/SaintBenedictParish/events/4979760 (March 12, 2016 video of a Saint Benedict Sunday homily, "Getting in the Game," by Fr. Simon)

Chapter 23 missionoftheredeemer.com (Michael Dopp's website, evangelization formation)
relittraining.com (DVD series teaching Catholics to share their faith hosted by Michael Dopp)
newevangelization.ca (annual Catholic New Evangelization Summit

companionscross.org/lay-formation/school-evangelization/talk-8-lords-dynamic (Fr. Bob Bedard video explaining the Lord's dynamic in evangelization) companionscross.org/homilies/fr-simon-lobo-cc/why-how-should-we-tell-others (March 31, 2016 audio recording of an Alpha talk by Fr. Simon) livestream.com/SaintBenedictParish/events/5166020 (April 10, 2016, video of a Saint Benedict Sunday homily, "To Suffer Dishonour," by Fr. Simon)

Chapter 24   studiobrien.com (books by Michael O'Brien). I recommend starting with the novel *Father Elijah*.) alpha.org, alphacanada.org, alphausa.org Search YouTube for the Alpha videos, especially the "Alpha Film Series." Search for the Divine Renovation podcasts on iTunes or SoundCloud. (Look for the three-part series "How to Kill Alpha in 10 Easy Steps.")

Chapter 25   htb.org (Holy Trinity Brompton Anglican Church, Alpha home base) stannparish.org (Saint Ann Catholic Parish, Coppell, Texas)

Chapter 27   madonnahouse.org (Madonna House offers opportunities for retreats and more.)

Chapter 29   John Maxwell, *Failing Forward: Turning Mistakes into Stepping Stones for Success*

Chapter 30   saintbenedict.ca/connect saintbenedict.ca/alpha saintbenedict.ca/saintbpserve

Chapter 31   Patrick Lencioni, *Death by Meeting: A Leadership*

Fable (reinvigorate a variety of meetings: Daily Check-in, Weekly Tactical, Monthly Strategic, and Quarterly Off-site Review)

Chapter 32   focus.org (Fellowship of Catholic University Students) Search YouTube for video explanations of spiritual multiplication.

Chapter 34   en.wikipedia.org/wiki/Four_stages_of_competence Just for fun, search online for "Opinionator Those Irritating Verbs as Nouns."

Chapter 35   divinerenovation.net/the_dr_network (more info and online application)

Chapter 38   siena.org (Catherine of Siena Institute Called and Gifted Workshop)
gallupstrengthscenter.com (CliftonStrengths Assessment)
Albert Winseman, Donald Clifton, Curt Liesveld, *Living Your Strengths: Discover Your God-Given Talents and Inspire Your Community (Catholic Edition)*
Art Bennett and Laraine Bennett, *The Temperament God Gave You*

Chapter 39   Henry Cloud and John Townsend, *Boundaries: When to Say Yes, How to Say No*
danreiland.com/delivering-the-answer-no-one-wants-to-hear
netcanada.ca/en (National Evangelization Teams of Canada)
netusa.org (National Evangelization Teams of the USA)

Appendix A

Other Resources on Evangelization, Parish Renewal, and Leadership

Papal Documents on Evangelization

Pope Francis, *Evangelii Gaudium (The Joy of the Gospel)*
Pope John Paul II, *Redemptoris Missio (The Mission of the Redeemer)*
Pope Paul VI, *Evangelii Nuntiandi (On Evangelization in the Modern World)*

Books on Evangelization

Fr. Raniero Cantalamessa, *Sober Intoxication of the Spirit*
Don Everts and Doug Schaupp, *I Once Was Lost*
Ralph Martin, *The Urgency of the New Evangelization*
Andre Regnier, *Catholic Missionary Identity*

Books on Parish Renewal

Lee Kricher, *For a New Generation*
Ed Stetzer and Mike Dodson, *Comeback Churches*
Graham Tomlin, *The Provocative Church*
Christopher Wesley, *Rebuilding Confirmation*
Christopher Wesley, *Rebuilding Youth Ministry*
Fr. Michael White and Tom Corcoran, *Rebuilding Your Message*
Fr. Michael White and Tom Corcoran, *The Rebuilt Field Guide*

Books on Leadership

Kenneth Blanchard and Spencer Johnson, *The One Minute Manager*
Bill Hybels, *Courageous Leadership*
Patrick Lencioni, *The Advantage: Why Organizational Health Trumps Everything Else in Business*
Andy Stanley, *Making Vision Stick*

Church Leadership Podcasts
>   Carey Nieuwhof Leadership Podcast (on iTunes, or go to
>   careynieuwhof.com/mypodcast)
>   Andy Stanley Leadership Podcast (on iTunes, or go to
>   andystanley.com/podcasts)

Church Leadership Blogs
>   Tony Morgan Live Blog (tonymorganlive.com/blog)

Acknowledgements

In addition to all of the people who feature in these reflections, the following people have also had a great impact on my life.

Mom and Dad: I love you! You were the first disciples to help foster my relationship with Jesus. Thank you for taking us to Saint Mary's in Ottawa where Fr. Bob Bedard was pastor and where I experienced a renewed parish for the first time as a child. Thank you for your constant example of serving and leading in the context of the parish and beyond.

My siblings (Jeremy, Naomi, and Ruth), your spouses, and your children: I am grateful that all of us are living as missionary disciples and that each of you have stepped up into leadership and ministries in your respective parishes, especially given the busyness of family life.

My brother Companions of the Cross (bishops, priests, and seminarians): you have all had an influence on my formation and my priesthood. Thanks especially to the brothers who took the time to encourage me as I sent out the original reflections and all who have gently guided me as a young priest and leader. Special thanks to Fr. Mark Goring for inviting me to accompany him on several writing (read: surfing) retreats. God has already used our modest little community in profound ways; I dream of the day when we will be blessing the broader Church through our expertise in evangelization, parish renewal, and leadership.

Saint Benedict Parish and so many others in the Archdiocese of Halifax-Yarmouth: I moved here only a few years ago and am clearly a CFA (Come From Away). Yet I have been welcomed and loved by several locals to the point that this place has really started to feel like home. Thanks to so many for your warm hospitality and love.

Maria Mellis, Vicki McEachern, and Brenton Cordeiro: at various points, you have each taken time to invest in me and help me develop as a writer. Thanks for all of the honest feedback—especially when I was not very good at receiving it.

Anne Louise Mahoney: your professional editing skills improved and polished the text, making it much more clear and readable. Thanks for cautioning me in certain areas while still allowing me to be myself. (I am particularly grateful that you gave in and let me keep the Bill Murray reference.)

Those who wrote endorsements: I appreciate your taking the time to read the manuscript and to offer many kind and affirming words. I asked each of you specifically because I respect your opinions and the impact that you are having on the Church.

Thanks to Jeff Smith, Beth McNamara, and the team at The Word Among Us for their support and their commitment to this project, and to Deacon Keith Strohm and Cindy Cavnar for their editorial assistance. Your gifted help brings this message to a broader audience.

At the risk of sounding like an NFL quarterback who just won the Super Bowl, I would like to give a shout-out to my personal Lord and Savior Jesus Christ. Looking back, I have no idea how I found the time, energy, or creativity to write these reflections. The biggest joke is that I never formally learned any English grammar. I don't read books as often as I want to; I have no business writing one. This entire work is because of God's free gift of grace. Thank you for my life. I feel that I have probably received more mercy and grace than most. I've probably needed more than most. Thank you for loving me without conditions. That's the best! I pray that every single person on the planet will have the opportunity to encounter Jesus' amazing life-changing love.

Divine Renovation Ministry

Are you and your parish ready to move from maintenance to mission?

You don't need to journey alone. The Divine Renovation Ministry coaches pastors and leadership teams as they take their parish from maintenance to mission. Visit www. divinerenovation.net to connect with the ministry and start the process of making joyful missionary disciples.

www.DivineRenovation.net